Where Grace Grows

Living in God's restoration,
love, and light.

His Grace shines as light in our darkness.

They will say, "This land that was laid waste
has become like the garden of Eden...."
Ezekiel 36:35 NIV

By: L. C. Boyd

Contributions by: Ben Plunkett
Cover photo by: Rebekah Plunkett

Heart felt thanks to
Cherri Brady and Chris Milom at Ideal Printing, Inc.
for their support, advice and sacrifice.

Table of Contents

Introduction

Jesus. His name alone shouts grace! It is because of his grace we are not consumed. Grace freely given, we do not deserve it. If we accept his gift of grace then we too are compelled to extend grace to others. Even the most difficult one we know, Jesus commands us to love them, pray for them, show grace to them. We cannot do all Jesus calls us to do without his strength. It is he who gives us the ability. He weeps for us. He prays for us. His spirit guides us. He is grace.

The only one who can cultivate my soul so deeply and allow His grace to grow in me, from what was once barren ground, is the Master Gardener himself, God of glory. He listens for the silent groans of our hurting hearts and He sees our affliction and He is moved with compassion for all of us.

Come and meet this precious Lord of Lords and King of Kings.

His name is Jesus and He cares about you. His grace is enormous! Unfortunately, some don't see it or even know about it. I wanted to write this book to help those who are hurting and in desperate need of his grace. To share with you how blessed I am to have been touched by His mercy and lifted up out of my sin on the wings of His forgiveness. He offers the same to you.

Through the journey of writing this book Jesus has taught me the lesson of forgiveness. He has flooded my heart with conviction at times, yet always covered in his mercy.

My prayer is that as you read this book you will realize His all sufficient grace, His infinite strength and His boundless love for you.

It takes effort and lots of prayer to follow Christ. There are times even now that I don't want to put forth the effort. I choose instead my own direction on a path that leads to anxious days and sleepless nights. There is no peace for the soul that wanders from the path that God has laid before them.

Be careful of detours you take. Prayerfully seek God's direction. Detours can take you completely away from God's planned course. In a direction you never imagined and further away from the God who loves you.

But if we seek God in all things He will be faithful to keep us on track. My heart's desire is to be the woman God calls me to be.

I pray your heart will be challenged and your life changed in some way for the glory of God. In the end, nothing else really matters.

> *Father, I thank you for your compassion and your patience. I pray your Spirit would flow through my hands and onto the pages of this book. I am nothing on my own. I pray your Spirit would speak to each heart reading these words and you would bless each heart far above anything any of us can imagine. May all the glory be yours Father. In Jesus' name, I pray.*

♦

Part I
A Tender Growth

Hope Out of Hurt

*"For I know the plans I have for you...plans to give
you hope and a future."*
Jeremiah 29:11 NIV

I. The Hurt of My Life

When I started this book of devotions, I didn't intend to write a book of sorrows and sadness. My deep desire was and still is to write words of encouragement and hope. But it has been through the sorrows and sadness of my life, I have learned to love God even more. I want to encourage those reading this book that God loves you and has a hope and a future for you.

My difficulties in life started very early. I grew up the child of an alcoholic. By the time I was sixteen I had experienced the separation and eventual divorce of my parents. My youth wasn't *all* bad. I have many sweet and precious memories which I will always cherish. But the drinking, fighting and the abuse my mom endured for years tend to mingle bitterness with the sweet.

Eventually dad left and the violence ended with his departure. Mom struggled to take care of six children on her own. We salvaged the pieces of our lives, but there was no time for dreaming as children like to do. We each had to fill a role in keeping the remnants of our family together.

Yes, there are unseen scars but more important is the healing that you *do* see. God has healed me through more blessings than I could ever imagine. Even in the most painful and deepest of despair God has always been there with me. Although it didn't seem very hopeful at the time, God was aware and He did not leave me. Indeed, He lifted me out of the ashes.

◆

II. Mending Your Heart

I dearly love my Dad. I do not write these words out of meanness or bitterness.

I believe there are many other adults who grew up as children of alcoholics. If you are one of them, I want to assure you there is hope for your hurt.

My dad passed away in 1998 and my oldest sister and I were with him until his last breath. I am grateful God brought us back together after so many years of separation. I am thankful God touched my dad's heart and by God's sweet grace my dad was forgiven and restored. On the day dad took his last breath on this earth he was welcomed into Heaven by our Lord Jesus. God is absolutely amazing isn't He?

I have tried to put these words on paper before, but I felt as though I were dishonoring the memory of my dad. Even now, as I am writing, the tears are falling and my entire body hurts for him.

God has touched my heart with His compassion. It is only God who is able to bring healing. I cannot begin to tell you of God's great mercy. He has not left me in my affliction. This is the God I want to share with you. Your hurt may be of a different kind, but God is the help you need. He will not leave you in your pain. He will speak peace to your heart, and cause beauty to bloom from the ashes of your despair. Jesus will always bring hope to those who hurt and who call out to Him.

♦

God Is Waiting To Bless You

"From the God of your father who helps you, and by the Almighty who blesses you with blessings of Heaven above."
Genesis 49:25 NASB

Where are you right now? Are you broken? Are you lonely? Do you have feelings of hopelessness? God can help. There has never been and never will be a person He cannot help.

God has an infinite supply of Himself to give. And in His great goodness He gives freely. Out of His infinite grace He gives much. He gives hope to the woefully undeserving. He gives new strength to those with no strength of their own. He causes blessings to flow like a mighty river.

God has invited us to enjoy this river. So what are you waiting for? Dive in! Plunge beneath His healing waters and emerge forgiven, restored and divinely blessed.

♦

Thinking of You

"...and when they heard that the Lord was concerned
about them and had seen their misery, they bowed
down and worshipped."
Exodus 4:31 NIV

On this quiet rainy morning
As I sit looking out the window
You come to my mind.

I believe God placed you in my thoughts
So I will be reminded to pray for you.

The prayers are being whispered;
God hears each one.
We both love you dearly.

♦

Suffering and Sorrow

"He was despised and rejected by mankind, a man of suffering,
and familiar with pain."
Isaiah 53:3 NIV

I. Honoring God in Pain

Yes each of us will experience some personal hurt or crisis during our lives, but God is *always* aware of our needs.

It looked like Job had lost everything in the world of any worth. Yet he continued to love the Lord no matter what. He remained fully committed to God even when it seemed he had lost everything. His wife even tried to turn Job against God, but Job remained steadfastly true to Him. You see, his trust in God was not superficial. Job obviously questioned why all this had come into his life—who of us wouldn't? But his love for God was deep and grounded. God brought him through his crisis, his desert experience, and blessed his life more than before his pain and loss.

In our times of crisis and affliction our true spiritual grit for God will be revealed. How will you react during hardship? Will you turn to Him in trust, believing He can right every wrong or will you cling to the hurt? Will you sling the pain over your shoulder, carrying it with you every hour of every day? In your heart are you secretly hoping that other people will feel sorry for you if you hold on to your problem long enough? I admit that I have done this. I am ashamed and I pray for God's forgiveness. These actions only bring conflict and dissention. God is not at all honored through such behavior.
How will you react?

II. The Isolation of Pain

Sometimes we choose to isolate ourselves when we are faced with a time of great personal struggle. This is not good, we need God and we need the prayers of others. Bitterness will begin to take root in our heart, stealing our joy and causing great emotional distress. God does not desire that we face life's challenges alone. Jesus knows our pain. He

5

suffered more pain on the Cross of Calvary than we can ever begin to comprehend. Why? Because He loves us so much He was willing to die for us. If He loves us enough to die for us don't you think He cares about our pain and suffering? We must choose to allow God to lift our burdens. We must let go of our pain and place it in God's hands before we can have healing and peace. Only His precious hands can undo the cord of sin that keeps us bound to our affliction and isolates us from our Lord. Anything that keeps us from God is sin.

We were meant to live victoriously through Jesus Christ. What holds you from this kind of life? What burdens your heart so deeply you cannot look up? Satan would have you keep believing you are not worthy of the grace God offers. Remember, God loves us so much He gave His only Son that whosoever believes on Him will not perish but have everlasting life. (John 3:16) No one else has ever loved us like that! And no one else ever will.

We are *never* told that conflict and crisis won't come knocking on our door. We will experience these times. We *are* told to place everything in His hands. Others will see God working and healing in our lives and it will bring glory to Him. We must not isolate ourselves from God's presence.

> *Father, whatever comes into my life this day I know You are aware and you have it under control. I do not need to live in isolation and fear. You are a God who knows. Nothing is hidden from You. Nothing touches my life except You allow it. You alone give the grace and strength to face it. I am never alone, for You are with me. During my long night You keep watch over me and in the morning you greet me. You are mighty and Your strength never fails. You bring hope and healing. You are my God and I praise You. You are very good to me, Father. Thank you. In Jesus' name, I pray.*

◆

Uncover My Heart

"He will gather His wheat into the barn,
but He will burn up the chaff..."
Matthew 3:12 NASB

Father, I have this chaff that covers my heart. I know it must be removed so that Your Holy Spirit can minister to me.

Father, I acknowledge the fact that you must spiritually crush me so that my outer husk can be removed. I know that only in this fashion can You reveal a tender and obedient heart in me.

I commit to being careful during these crushing times. They are never pleasant and can have the opposite of the ideal response. If I do not turn to You for guidance during these times, they can make me bitter and cause me to be separated from you.

I pray that they will instead cause me to fall into Your arms of protection, covered by Your grace and drawn closer to You.

Father, I pray my heart will be tender to Your words. I pray that each grain of Your mercy, forgiveness and love will fall into the prepared soil of my heart and multiply.

Thank You for seeing past the outer shell of me and seeing a useful servant in the heart of me.

I praise Your name!

◆

Momma's Warm Cake

"The people of Israel called the bread manna. It was white like coriander seed and tasted like wafers made with honey."
Exodus 16:31 NIV

We all have sweet memories tucked away in our mind. These are treasured pieces of our past. As I've gotten older I have realized the need to let go of those things that held me captive and stole my joy. Instead, I choose to cling to these memories that make me smile.

I remember momma making hot chocolate. It was not one of these "instant" deals. It was homemade and it was delicious! But my very favorite treat was her baked cake. She would put the frosting on it while it was still warm and then we would indulge in this sweet satisfaction. Everyone should experience the delight of eating warm cake with melted frosting. And it is always best when accompanied by a glass of cold milk. (Can you say "yum"?)

No matter how much I try to describe this cake, you will never know the sweet satisfaction it gives unless you try it for yourself. The same is true with our divine relationship. You can hear people talk about God every day, but until you meet Him and taste the sweetness of His Word you can never truly experience the joy He offers.

God is good. And the best part is that unlike a cake, God remains forever. He has an endless supply of Himself for us to enjoy! God's love for us falls like manna from the sky. He never runs out of His blessings and forgiveness. God is warm, inviting, never cold, and never unapproachable. He is truly good all of the time.

Until you meet God and sample what He has to offer, you will never know the delight that awaits you. He is Jesus, the sweetest of all joys, sweeter than honey from out of the comb, yes, even sweeter than Momma's cake!

◆

Sweet Waters

"When they came to Marah, they could not drink the waters of Marah, for they were bitter..."
Exodus 15:23 NASB

Just three days after the miraculous parting of the Red Sea, the Israelites grumbled about the bitter waters of Marah. Although the people complained against God, Moses prayed for them and God provided a way to turn the bitter waters sweet. God didn't stop there. He also led them to Elim where there were multiple springs of water, date palms, and places to rest.

This story reminds us of the truth that God hears our prayers. If all we do is grumble instead of praying and seeking God's face, we miss the blessings He has for us.

I doubt that anyone will deny that life can be very unpleasant at times. We will encounter Marah-like bitterness in our own lives. We will experience bitter moments because we live in a sinful world.

There is good news! God knows. He waits for us to call out and He comes to our rescue. You have a choice. You can go directly to God or you can grumble your way right out of His blessing.

Job 2:10 asks: *"Shall we indeed accept good from God and not accept adversity?"*

God does not want to hear us grumbling, He wants us to be faithful to Him in both good times and bad.

Will you allow God to work through you even in the bad times? Will you allow God to use you as an instrument to lead others to brighter places? Moses did. Through God's power he led thousands of people through a sea on dry ground. By the power of God, he provided the people with drinkable water. Through God's guidance, he led them to a place of rest.

What holds you back from enjoying God's blessing? We will never see past our difficulties if all we do is grumble. It is only when we decide to glorify God in every experience of our lives that we can truly experience His blessing.

Father, I ask You to turn my bitterness into your sweetness. Bless my life with the fruit of Your hands. Give me rest at Your peaceful oasis. I thank You and praise You for the mercy You show me daily. I pray every thirsty soul will come to drink from the sweet fountain of life. Jesus, You are our Fountain of Living Water. In Jesus' name I pray.

♦

Only from a Distance

*"...because both of you broke faith with me...because
you did not uphold my holiness. Therefore you will see
the land only from a distance you will not enter the
land I am giving to the people of Israel"*
Deuteronomy 32:51-52 NIV

It seems harsh when you read God's judgment on Moses
and his brother Aaron, after they had spent all those years
leading thousands of people out of Egypt and into freedom
from captivity. Moses endured great hardship and adversity
directly caused by those he was trying to help. During his
lifetime of ministry, Moses would travel many miles, face
numerous obstacles, and lead thousands of people through
harsh lands on their way to God's Promised Land.

During their captivity, God's people had suffered deep
affliction at the hands of the Egyptians. You would think they
would be joyful at having these burdens lifted. You want to
believe they had complete obedience to the God who saved
them. But no, at the first sign of conflict they wanted to run
back to the very ones who held them in bondage. How much
are we like that? I know I am. God forgive me.

In a moment of human weakness, Moses and Aaron
sinned against God's directions for them. Because of this
disobedience, they were both denied entrance into the land
they were longing to see. They would have no part in leading
the children of Israel into their promised land.

God's action here may seem excessively hard, but in
reality it drives home the seriousness of obeying our holy
God. He specifically chose and commanded Moses in this
position of leadership. And since he was in a position of
leadership, God expected much of him.

The same is true of us today. A man or woman in a
position of leadership is held at a higher standard. Many eyes
are focused on their work, many ears tuned to what they say.

Moses and Aaron continued to lead God's people to their appointed destination. However, due to the consequences of their sin they would not be allowed to enter this land of rest. But because He is a loving God, He would lead Moses up into a mountain where he could see the land from a distance. How sad to be so close but to lose God's blessing of entering His promised land.

We should not take lightly our responsibility in any area of service to the Lord. God demands our highest respect and obedience when we are called to do a job for Him. You may be called to care for little ones in the nursery or to scrub fingerprints from walls or to teach young hearts. God takes all of His work seriously.

How sad if at the end of our journey He finds that we have only served Him halfheartedly, having chosen instead our own way of doing things. When my journey has ended I anticipate the joy of entering God's promised land of Heaven. There I will forever see him face to face not from a distance.

◆

Going Home

"...She left the place where she had been living and set out on the road that would take them back to the land of Judah"
Ruth 1:7 NIV

I. Far from Home

Naomi and her family were transplanted Israelites living in Moab. They had traveled there years earlier because of a famine in their homeland of Israel. After the death of her husband and two sons, Naomi heard the news that God had come to the help of His people in Israel (Ruth 1:6). Naomi longed to return home, back to her comfort zone, back to her friends, and extended family, back to the land she knew. After all, she had nothing to keep her in the land in which she was living. She was probably lonely and longed for the comfort and company of her own people. We are all like that, at least a little bit. In times of loneliness and isolation, we reach out for the familiar, the presence of someone who can comfort us. We miss the comfort of home.

We know that Naomi was not emotionally and possibly spiritually well because she later requests to be called Mara, meaning bitter, instead of Naomi (verse 20). Maybe it was because she was away from her homeland. Being apart from God can make us bitter as well. When we wander from the path God has planned for us, we too will lose our joy.

But God can turn us around. He offers grace, forgiveness, and restoration. I urge you to prayerfully make your choices. Naomi chose the road that took her back to her homeland.

I can relate to Naomi's story. Whenever I read it, I imagine myself in her sandals. I can remember many times when I left my sweet land of communion with God. I selfishly chose to go where I thought the grass was greener. But when I got there, I found the land was full of mourning and discontent. That is not the kind of place God desires for His children. It is not the full life in Christ God desires for us to have.

13

I have never found contentment or joy when choosing my own way. It sometimes happens that I experience feelings of relief or temporary happiness. However, in time these feelings fade into despair. When these feelings of despair arrive, I find myself longing for what only God can give. In such times, my soul aches to go back to my homeland, the sweet land of plenty—back to God.

II. The Hard Road Back

Walking with the Lord is not always easy. We will still face challenges. We will experience difficulties that are beyond our control. No matter what happens, we must cling to the faithfulness and infinite love of God.

Nowhere in the Bible does God promise us a life completely free of trials and heartache. He does, however, promise to walk with us every step of the way. He promises He will be with us, listening for our prayers. God will welcome His children back with open arms when they seek His mercy and forgiveness.

Naomi may have left her home land but God did not refuse to accept her back.

As Naomi made her way back down the streets of her hometown, the whole town was talking (Ruth 1:19). I want to believe that even though she said "call me Marah" she could feel the bitterness slowly ebbing away. She was coming home!

When one is about reach home after being gone for some time, it is a welcome sight when we see the lights of our destination ahead. God is the light that draws us home to quiet rest in Him. If you have traveled far from home, you should not remain there. We must always remember God will come to our aid. He has sent you a Savior and Guide to bring you home safely. If you are away from God right now, do not delay in returning to Him.

God continued to bless Naomi. Later He gave her a grandson by her faithful daughter-in-law Ruth. He restored her joy and renewed her life. Take the time to read for yourself this beautiful story of forgiveness, grace and restoration. God is the same today as He was then. He remains a God of compassion who waits, ready to welcome His children home.

♦

Rest

"The Lord Your God will give you rest by giving you this land."
Joshua 1:13 NIV

God's promise of rest is as true for us today as it always has been for every child of God. He *is* our rest. We spend our lives wandering in a desert of emotional or physical afflictions, ongoing illnesses, difficult relationships, and death. But God promises to bring us one day into His heavenly land of peace and promise. The only stipulations are that we love Him, seek His forgiveness, trust Him, and obey His commands.

He is rest for our weariness. I am so thankful and I Praise Him!

Have you ever felt so hopeless you could not get out of bed? You just could not face another day at your job, or endure another minute of your difficult marriage? You cry out to God when you're unable to stand on your own. He gives strength when you are spiritually weary. He knows when you are physically drained and He cares that you struggle. He knows the pain you have and He has compassion. God will always be true to give you rest. He will lift that yoke of affliction. He will welcome you into His land of peace and promise. He will take care of and provide for you.

God promises to provide the strength we need to endure if we call upon Him.

Lord, many times you've led me up a mountain,
guided by the strength of your hand.
But when life's trials and tears rain down upon me,
I am often frightened and run away again.

Many mornings I'd find you waiting
When I fell on my face in prayer;
Your presence filled my heart to overflowing,
Your glory shined through my deep despair.

In your strength alone I face this day's journey.
When I am faint, I know you carry me,
Embraced by the loving arms of Jesus—
In what sweeter place could I ever be?

♦

Altar

"....I will go to the altar of God..."
Psalm 43:4 NASB

Remember teaching your children how to walk? Remember how you guided them through each little step. The same is true with you and God. But the first step is up to you. You must choose to take that first step to God your Father.

*At this same altar years ago, you came in prayer for
your father.
What has changed that you can't come now to pray
for yourself and others?
Was it because as a little boy your heart was young
and tender?
You felt the hand of God so sweet and in obedience
surrendered.
Has that same heart become so cold, it cannot feel
God's spirit plead?
What keeps you from coming to the Savior when His
touch is all you need?
Has it been so long you have forgotten the way?
Are the steps too hard to take?
Lift up your eyes; do not delay; the path to the altar
is straight.
I know in my heart God feels your pain,
He holds your life in His hands.
He pleads today as He did when you were young,
Though now you've become a man.
Remember how you helped teach your son to walk?
He took one step then another.
The same is true with God and you,
You must take that first step toward God your
Father.*

◆

Father, I know many times Your Spirit has moved upon my heart. When it did, I confess I have sometimes gripped the pew to keep from stepping out and walking to the altar. You knew the struggle within my heart. Your Spirit urged me to come and worship you and lift up my prayers to you—but I stood by and lost that opportunity. Yes, I know we can worship you anywhere, but there is something intimate about meeting with you at the altar of prayer. It is a place set aside to kneel before you in Holy Communion. It is an actual, physical place where we can lay down our troubles and pain or lift up offerings of praise to you, Father. How many lives have been changed at the altar? We may never know until we reach heaven. Our family was held together by the prayers of one that knelt at your altar. Others met him there and began to pray as well. You heard their prayers Father and lives have been forever changed because of it. You alone are worthy to be praised. Forgive me for the times your Spirit has moved upon my heart and I did not heed your call to come to the altar. I know I missed a blessing and I may have caused someone else to miss one as well. I pray you will never cease to draw us to your altar of prayer. Thank you Father. In Jesus' name I pray.

◆

We're Not Paper Dolls

"My soul yearns, even faints, for the courts of the Lord;
my heart and my flesh cry out for the living God."
Psalm 84:2 NIV

When I was a little girl I remember playing with paper dolls. I was thinking the other day how I sometimes dress myself like one of those dolls. In other words, I sometimes pretend to be something I'm not. Allow me to explain.

1. **I get dressed**. Poking through my closet I try to piece together an outfit for the day. In this way I choose an outfit for the outer me—something that covers my flaws and imperfections. If I feel good about the outer me I can mask how I feel on the inside.

   I usually decide to wear a pretty shirt. This is frequently bright-colored and cheerful. This kind of shirt tends to make me feel good about myself and helps me cover my pain. I say to myself: *"I can get through one more day if I just pick the right top. Covering up my sins is a lot easier than confessing them. I will just pull this new shirt over them and get through one more day."*

   Occasionally, I will wear a skirt, but most of the time you will see me in pants. I like the jeans that are loose in the hips where I carry a little extra baggage! Speaking of baggage, most of us have a lot of it in our lives. I'm specifically talking about those things we're not quite ready to let go of just yet. Daily I pull on this "old baggage" along with my "loose fit" jeans and drag myself out the door. I may be struggling, but I can play the part for eight hours or so. No problem, right?

2. **I put on my happy face**. I may be struggling to keep it together but a little blush on those droopy cheeks adds color and can make me appear to have a glow. This will mask my current worries. Then no

20

one needs to be bothered with my feelings. I can play this part well.

3. **I make sure my hair is just right**. If you are like me you have bad hair days often! On these days you really need a cap to hide the mess. My hair reminds me of those little thoughts that mess with my mind—hard to get under control. These thoughts often involve memories of past bad choices which lead to overwhelming regret. Such thoughts steal my joy and keep me "tangled" in misery. I just grab a cap or a bandana—no one will ever know the difference. I know there are others out there with the same "bad hair" days.

God's Word tells us in Ephesians 4:22-25 to put off your old self which is being corrupted by its deceitful desires. Instead we must choose to be made new in the attitude of your mind by putting on the new self. As such a new creature, we will be re-created to be like God in true righteousness and holiness. As united members of the body of Christ, we must reject all falsehood and speak truthfully!

God sees our hearts. He knows we all hurt and have regrets. However, He does not want us to treat ourselves like paper dolls, covering up our hurts and our scars. Instead, He wants to heal them and make us new and alive in Him. We're beautiful children of God created for His glory.

Father, You are precious to me. You have created each of us with Your loving and gentle hands. Your Spirit is alive in us. You breathed into us life and feelings and emotions. We are far from being paper dolls. You have created us to be beautiful people for your glory. With our lips we praise you. There is no God besides You. You are amazing. Oh how good and lovely You are. I love You, Jesus. I thank You for Your forgiveness of my sins and removing the rags of my depravity. No paper outfits for me! With your hands you cover me. You alone are to be praised. Thank You, Father of all creation. In Jesus' name I pray.

◆

Early Morning Prayer

"...In the morning my prayer comes before you."
Psalms 88:13 NIV

Precious heavenly Father, as I opened my eyes this morning my thoughts were on you. I may be unsure of the path that I walk, but I know that you take every step of it with me. You are so good to me. We have shared laughter and tears, hope and healing. When my path is dark, when the waves of doubt roll over me You are there. When I reach up my hands for You, You rescue me. You carry me in Your strong arms.

Father, I love you. I am grateful and humbled that the God of the universe hears me when I cry out to him. As a mother runs to her crying child, you are swift to hear my prayers. You never leave me. Heaven and earth give witness to your greatness. I join them in songs of praise to you, God of glory. In Jesus' name I pray.

♦

Growing a Servant

"Truly I am your servant, LORD;...You have freed me from my chains."
Psalms 116:16 NIV

I pray for the strength to endure this time of suffering and pain. I pray for the faith to hold on to God while letting go of everything else. All that I need is God. His grace is indeed sufficient. His peace transcends all understanding. His joy is complete.

If you are struggling at this moment, lift up your eyes to God. When there is no clear path, when your eyes are blurred by tears of rejection and sorrow, hold tight to the One who holds you.

Be still this hour and feel the presence of the Lord. He is with you. He is faithful. He will be your light on this dark path you find yourself on. Trust Him to carry you through. It is through our struggles we come to know our Lord intimately. In His strength we are made strong. Hang in there! Your blessing waits just on the other side of your complete surrender to the One who surrendered His life for you.

God, there is no other like you. You are lovely and amazing. You are an awesome God. You are wonderful. I thank you for your deep compassion and love for me. I come before your throne of mercy with a broken and humbled heart. Father, you began this good work. I stand amazed at your kindness to me. I know and trust you to bring sweet victory from my struggles. Thank you, God of glory. In Jesus' name I pray.

♦

You are Priceless

"...her worth is far above jewels."
Proverbs 31:10 NASB

Every woman can reap a harvest of instruction from Proverbs 31. God wants us to read His Word and apply it to our lives. He wants us to know how special we are to Him. He wants us to discover His desire for us. He is so concerned with us because human beings are the pinnacle of His creation. We are worth far more than the most precious jewels. We are worth so much, in fact, that we are priceless.

He, therefore, has high expectations of us. He wants us to be trustworthy. He wants us to act kindly and lovingly to one another. He wants us to keep ourselves from evil. He wants us to be ready and willing to help those around us. He wants us to be diligent in everything we do at work, home, or outside the home. He wants us to be modest in dress because it matters to God how we present ourselves. He wants us to be faithful stewards of our finances. He wants us to give with a cheerful heart. (Know, though, that it is impossible for us to out give God. God returns every blessing many times over when we give with a willing and loving attitude.)

Sisters we need to be women of noble character. This nobility includes wisdom, but this definitely does not mean one should be a know-it-all. Sometimes wisdom and nobility of character are exhibited best by our silence. We must exercise caution, because hurtful words can never be taken back after they are spoken. God does not delight in gossip or idle talk. We should always speak with kindness and love. (I confess I need more of the Master's touch here!) A noble person is a beautiful person in God's eyes. When we are open to His teaching our outer woman will exhibit this inner beauty. We gain this beauty by daily walking with Him. When we live God's way, the things we do and say will not go unnoticed. And this beauty displayed in our lives will reflect well on God and our families.

A word about the wife working outside the home: I speak as a wife who does. It does not give us a "free pass" to neglect our families. It is often hard to give your work and your family full attention, but it can be done. But of the two, the family is vastly more important.

Wives, our families need our own special touch. They deserve the best we have to offer. A drive-thru meal is a nice occasional treat, but it should not replace good home cooking! (Yes, I do drive thru too!)

Being the wife and mother God wants us to be requires not being lazy. We must rise early to prepare ourselves for the day. We absolutely *must* have a daily quiet time with God. We must take a lead role in preparing our families for the day. Be a mother and wife your family can truthfully call a blessing from God.

Sisters, we will excel in all that we do if God is in it. He has blessed His creation with beauty and charm. Our love for the Lord makes us all the more beautiful, because He is beautiful. Therefore, with our hands, our hearts, and our minds let us live to serve Him. Our daily prayer should therefore be to have hearts that beat for God.

◆

A Cord of Many

"Though one may be overpowered, two can defend themselves.
A cord of three strands is not quickly broken."
Ecclesiastes 4:12 NIV

This devotion will require your imagination:

First, imagine I have a hand full of threads.

Second, imagine I am holding up one of the threads. This one thread alone represents me. It's pretty easy to break a single thread. Alone I too am weak.

Third, imagine three more threads joined to the single thread. These four joined threads represent the fortress we receive in God. When we become His we begin to grow in spiritual, physical and emotional strength. We need God! We need prayer! We need each other!

Fourth, imagine I am tying these four strings together. This represents the unity found in the body of believers and God is the strength that holds us securely together.

Fifth, imagine I am now intertwining or braiding them together. When this is finished they are held together in a cord that will not easily come apart. Together, we will not be easily broken. Remember, you are not left alone to face your uncertain future. You are one of many beautiful strands woven into a strong cord and held by God's hand. You can even become stronger by daily adding threads of love, compassion, forgiveness and mercy. Ephesians 4:3 (NIV) says, *"Make every effort to keep the unity of the Spirit through the bond of peace."* Let us stay unified! My heart beats with anticipation of what God can and will do in our lives as we humbly seek Him and pray for each other.

♦

Father, often we hold on to our struggles as if they were priceless treasure. Forgive us, Father. Our worries and fears and feelings of insecurities are just rags covering our sin of faithlessness in you. We hide behind the excuse that we have nothing to offer. Satan is so proud to have us as his guest at his table of discouragement. Father, we desire more. We long to feast at your banquet table, to sample the sweet manna of your word. We desire to serve you with the gifts and abilities you have given to each of us. Interwoven into a cord of strength and tied by your hands we will bind our families to you. God may we be the spark that ignites the flames of service not just here at Bethel but in our homes and community. Alone we are weak, but a cord of many is not easily broken. We can rest securely in your hands knowing you are the One who keeps us held together. Thank you, Father. You are good in all your ways and we love you. In Jesus' name I pray.

◆

I Have Seen Him

"In the year that King Uzziah died, I saw the Lord..."
Isaiah 6:1 NIV

I. Purify My Heart

Isaiah was a prophet of God. He preached about God. But when Isaiah came into the presence of God in a vision he was brought face to face with his own sinfulness.

But God did not leave Isaiah at that place of brokenness. Verse 7 tells us that at the touch of God his sins were forgiven and atoned for. In the presence of a Holy God Isaiah realized his need for a touch from the Lord. He needed to be cleansed from his sin and to feel the touch of the Master. In order for Isaiah to do the work the Lord called him to do, he needed to have a pure heart. When God calls us we too need to serve with a pure heart. We must be cleansed by the purifying touch of God.

II. Living His Will

When God says: "whom shall I send? And who will go for us" (Verse 8)? Isaiah answers: "here am I, send me".

I recall many times I have said those very words. I felt in my heart I meant it when I said them. God knows my heart. He knows there are times I follow Him from a distance, although I desire to be closer to Him. Just in these past months God has become more to me than words spoken. I have seen Him, in faith, working in the hearts and lives of His people and yes even me. I can say as Isaiah did in verse 5: "Woe is me, for I am ruined! Because I am a man (woman) of unclean lips...." Oh God how thankful I am that you do not leave us where you find us. Father not my lips only, but all of me.

God, forgive me and cleanse me of my sin. With my heart, and not in word only, I cry out: "Here I am, Send me!"

♦

Celebration Prayer

"Sing to the Lord for He has done glorious things."
Isaiah 12:5 NIV

Father, you have blessed us with good friends and family. My heart rejoices. It is good to see our children happy and blessed.

Prior to this wonderful day we as a family experienced a time of drought. Our hearts were parched as the hottest desert. We have visited and tasted the bitter waters of Marah.

But through every moment You Father have remained faithful. You have brought new joy to our hearts and put a new song on our lips. We sing songs of praise to the God of our salvation.

My heart rejoices to see the blessings you have bestowed on us this day. I am full of the goodness of the Lord and my cup is over flowing. You have supplied every need. You are a God who cares. You have come to our rescue and you alone lift our burdens.

God of heaven, your goodness to us is humbling and your mercy is great. You alone deserve all praise and glory.

In Jesus' name I pray.

♦

God Knows Me

"I have called you by name; you are mine!"
Isaiah 43:1 NASB

As you read what God says in this verse, picture yourself literally present as God speaks these precious words. He tells us a lot about Himself: He tells us that He created us, that He formed us, that He knows us individually, and that He calls us by name.

God is our strength and protection. He has always made a way for His children and has been their strength.

He is the Lord our God, the Holy One, our Savior. Apart from Him there is no Savior. We are precious, loved and honored in His sight. We need not fear because He is with us.

He is our Father. We are His sons and daughters, called by His name, and created for His glory. He has always made a way for His children and has been their provider.

He is our sovereign Lord. No one can pluck us from His hand.

He is our Redeemer, our Creator, and our King.

He is the Living Water.

Let us praise the Lord God!

His love never ceases to amaze me.

If you do not know this blessed Savior what keeps you from falling before Him now in prayer of repentance? Can it be any clearer how much God cares for you? All through His Word He reminds us of His great compassion for us. Over and over He extends mercy and grace and forgiveness. God waits for us to confess with our mouth that He is Lord.

He is whispering to you. Can you hear Him? He is pleading with you to repent of and forsake your sins. In obedience and trust we must choose to live for Him and accept His offer of salvation.

When God's Spirit whispers your name will you be listening? He has made a way for you to come to Him. The only way is through His Son Jesus who died on the cross for our sins.

Listen quietly. Is God calling your name?

♦

My Devastation, God's Deliverance

"It is good to wait quietly for the salvation of the Lord."
Lamentations 3:26 NIV

I am not a quiet spirit and I struggle with waiting. Though I struggle, God is with me during the times I am appointed to wait.

Just prior to this passage in verse 25 we are told that *"the Lord is good to those who hope in him."* I claim that promise and hold tight to it. I couldn't even crawl out of bed each day if I didn't have Him as my hope. Yes, I will continue to cling to the Lord of my hope.

Later in verse 32 we are reminded that, *"Though He brings grief, He will show compassion, so great is His unfailing love."* I find strength and peace knowing that though the storms of adversity sweep over my life, my Hope, my God will bring deliverance. He is my salvation. My Lord is indeed strong.

In verse 33 we are told He does not willingly bring affliction or grief to the children of men. It is because of the sins of man that we even experience difficulty of any kind. But God does not leave us to face our grief and burdens on our own or in our own strength. Our strength comes from the Lord. Philippians 4:13 (NIV) assures us that *"I can do all this through him who gives me strength."* God's massive power is only a prayer away from any need we have. He is our strength and deliverer.

In verse 57 of this chapter God's Word brings us comfort when we are reminded that *our Lord came near when we called. He came with gladness, spoke to our hearts and told us not to fear.*

We do not serve a God of fear or hopelessness. Our God is a God who knows and cares more deeply for us than we can imagine. He joyfully hears when we call His name.

Imagine a child calling out to her daddy who quickly comes and bends down to look into her face. God our heavenly Father is exactly the same with us His children. Like a rebellious child, I still struggle with being fully sold out to God. Many times I cry out, questioning God. But when I sit in quiet prayer and lay my burdens before His throne of mercy, His grace flows over me and my joy is full in Him.

I have lost count of the times God has delivered me from life's struggles. I know He will be faithful to keep me safe through this journey of life. His mercy has been extended to me; His grace covers me; I am truly blessed to know Him as my eternal Lord and Savior. Will you join me? He is the Lord of our salvation.

◆

We Are One in Spirit

"I will give you a new heart and put a new spirit in you..."
Ezekiel 36:26 NIV

If you are a child of the King of glory, His spirit resides in you. When you accepted Jesus as your Savior and Lord, His Spirit immediately filled your heart and soul. And since we have the Spirit of God in us, nothing should hinder us from serving Him and loving others. We lose out on the abundant life because we settle for the least when we can have the most and best of God.

I desire to know and cherish every blessing God has for me. He promises, if we are faithful and obedient to Him, He will throw open the floodgates of heaven and pour out so much blessing that we will not have room enough for all of it.

When God pours out blessings it isn't less than the best. It is heavenly blessings. I do not want anyone to think for a moment that the only reason to serve God is for His blessings. If we never receive another gift at all His greatest gift was more than enough. It is the gift of His son Jesus through whom the whole world can obtain forgiveness of sin and life eternal in Heaven.

We miss out on so much that God wants to do in us when we fail to live obediently. I'm not saying I'm perfect in this regard. I have a problem with this too.

God knows our heart and He knows every need and desire of our heart. 1 John 5:14-15 (NIV) says, *"This is the confidence we have in approaching God: that if we ask anything according to His will, He hears us."* Notice the phrase, *"according to His will."* God knows what is best for us and we must trust Him. Even when the path is dark and your steps are unsteady hold tight to Him and trust Him to lead you.

Have you ever eaten from a buffet? One price and you can eat as much as you desire. God's banquet table is prepared. He calls His children; come home and come in, be filled and be satisfied. Hunger no more for He is the Bread of life. Thirst no more for He is the Living Water. God can and will fill your spiritual cup to overflowing. God bids us come to him empty and He will fill us. He will provide for our every need. His Son Jesus has already paid your debt. Now all you need to do is enter in, pull up your chair and spend eternity enjoying sweet communion with our Lord and Savior. This is the blessing I love with all my heart!

Praise the God of Glory!

Lord, You prepare a table before me, You anoint my head with oil; my cup overflows. Surely goodness and loving-kindness will follow me all the days of my life, and I will dwell in the House of the Lord forever.
Psalm 23:5&6

◆

God Is Able

"....your friends will deceive and overpower you; those who eat your bread will set a trap for you, but you will not detect it...The day of the Lord is near for all nations. As you have done, it will be done to you; your deeds will return upon your own head."
Obadiah 1:7&15 NIV

God's Word is true and living and faithful to keep all of its promises. His Word does not return void. Whatever He speaks is so. And God is aware of everything we encounter. Sometimes it appears that evil has the upper hand in the world. It seems that it will triumph. However, God says "as you have done, it will be done to you." I believe that means that our own actions whether good or evil will be repaid us.

That is why all of our actions should be centered in God. He alone is able to make all things right. This means when you experience anger or bitterness or a desire for revenge that you *must* pray your way through these feelings. You may feel justified in these feelings due to the actions of those who hurt you, but all of it is *sin*. You and I must commit our hurts and deepest feelings of rejection to God. He will cause the deeds of those who hurt you, to return upon their heads.

Always remember that God is faithful. He will give you hope and the strength you need to move past your hurt. Know that in the end He will make right what is wrong.

Trust in the Lord always.

♦

The Night Is Over

"The night is nearly over the day is almost here. So let us put aside the deeds of darkness and put on the armor of light."
Romans 13:12 NIV

My night has passed. The crying of the night hours has ceased. God has blessed me with a new day. He has granted peace. He has not forsaken me. I will praise Him for being with me through this journey:

I praise Him for patiently waiting for me to return to Him. I praise Him for His bountiful grace, compassion and loveliness. I praise His steadfast love and constant presence in my life.

I find more reason to praise Him with every passing day.

I have so many reasons to be thankful to God. Most of all I am eternally grateful for His forgiveness. He has forgiven me so much. Because of Him, my night has turned into a blessed new day. I praise Him for this new life that He has given me. I will rejoice and be glad in Him.

I will thank him with my whole heart. Yes, I will rejoice in His everlasting goodness and eternal blessings.

The Son of God has risen victorious in my heart. He is the Light in my darkness. I am blessed to call Him Lord.

♦

Part II
Blooms of Beauty

Where Grace Blooms

*"The desert and the parched land will be glad; the
wilderness will rejoice and blossom."*
Isaiah 35:1 NIV

I. In the Desert

I ran into the desert to escape the pain and the adversity
of my life. Jesus found me there. In my great distress, He
came to my rescue. In a dry and barren land God met me.
He spoke to my heart and encouraged me by His presence.
He lifted me up and set me on a path toward healing.

God was waiting for me when I ran to Him. God's mercy
flowed into my heart, like water into a dry desert.

God's mercy is rooted deeply in His love for us. His grace
will bloom in the hearts of those who seek Him.

When we run into the desert to escape the pain, when our
heart cries out for relief, it is there we can say as Hagar so
long ago… "You are the God who sees me…I have now seen
the One who sees me." (Genesis 16:13 NIV). Praise Him!

The story of Hagar is found in Genesis 16. Hagar was the
Egyptian servant who bore a son to Abraham as a part of
Sarah's plan to have a child.

This only brought conflict, causing Hagar to be
mistreated by a jealous Sarah. In her great distress Hagar
ran into the dry, barren desert. There she added physical
suffering to her already great emotional suffering. But God
saw her there. He heard her cries. He was there waiting when
she stopped running.

God has not changed since the time of Hagar. He
continues to meet us at our place of deepest need. He is more
than a stream where we find rest when we feel we can go no
further. If you read on in verse 14 you will find that Hagar
finds a well called Beer Lahai Roi ("the well of the Living
One"). No longer just a stream to rest beside, Hagar has
found the well of the living One. A well in the dry desert—
that's God! God is altogether amazing and wonderful! He is
the well of the living One! Praise Him!

41

But there is more. God's blessing continued. After He met with her at the well, Hagar later gave birth to a son. As God commanded she named him Ishmael ("God Hears") verse 11. So every time Hagar spoke her son's name she was reminded of the day she met God in her desert of affliction and remembered that He is a God who hears.

I really love this story. My heart is spilling over as I type these words!

Oh, how wonderful God is! Praise Him!

Our God is alive! Our God hears! Our God heals!

II. Out of the Desert

God knew there would be others like Hagar. Fortunately, God has not changed. His ear is always listening for the cries of those who call out to Him in their time of need. He is the stream we can rest beside. He is the well of living water where the thirstiest soul can be quenched. He has delivered into the barren wasteland of mankind the everlasting well of His Son Jesus Christ.

His tender mercy brings renewed hope. We can now love others because the love of God is in us through Jesus. God's grace continues to grow in the hearts of those His hand has touched. We can never be the same after that!

Father, I thank you for hearing me when I cried out to you. You have given me hope and covered my heart with your peace. My affliction was great, my burden was heavy and I had no rest. You have lifted my burden and caused me to be able to stand. I have found rest with you. You, Father, are my well of living water, I will never thirst again. By your grace I have life and it is a life abloom where once was only barrenness. You are good in all your ways and I love you. I pray for all those who struggle, who are fainting under their pain and burdens. God touch their heart, meet them in their desert journey and quench their thirsty souls. You alone can meet every need and bring blessing from their hurt. You are truly a God who sees. I pray that we can say as Hagar did, "I have now seen the One who sees me." All glory to you Father of Heaven and earth. In Jesus' name I pray.

♦

Freedom for the Captives

*"Now the Lord is the Spirit, and where the
Spirit of the Lord is, there is freedom."*
2 Corinthians 3:17 NIV

Prison bars are not the only things that hold us captive!
We are held in Satan's grip, a bondage that tightens as long
as we do not confess and forsake our sins. Jesus came to
proclaim freedom for the captives. That includes you and me.
We are called to be servants of Christ rather than sin. What
holds you in captivity? Of what are you a prisoner? What is it
that keeps you in bondage and keeps you from enjoying
freedom in Christ?

Even after I accepted Christ as my Savior, I lived with the
guilt and humiliation of my past sinful lifestyle. I *wanted* to
live a life of joy, but I always ended up carrying my old
baggage with me. The weight of the past held me down and
prevented me from looking up and seeing Christ with His
arms out stretched ready to lift by burden.

God's Word gave me hope. In John 10:9-10 Jesus says to
us: "I am the gate; whoever enters through me will be saved.
He will come in and go out and find pasture. The thief comes
only to steal and kill and destroy; I have come that they may
have life, and have it to the full.

If Christ has forgiven us we are told in His Word that He
wants us to have a full life. Not a life hidden in shame. Satan
would have us live our lives in his shadow of misery and
defeat. But I will remind you that Jesus has already defeated
Satan. He conquered death and Hell on the Cross of Calvary.

In Revelations 12:9&10 (NIV) we are given a symbolic
picture of what happened: The great dragon was hurled
down-that ancient serpent called the devil, or Satan, who
leads the whole world astray. He was hurled to the earth, and
his angels with him.

Then I heard a loud voice in heaven say: "*Now have come
the salvation and the power and the kingdom of our God,
and the authority of His Messiah. For the*

44

accuser of our brothers and sisters, who accuses them before our God day and night, has been hurled down." Praise the Lord!

Do you see what God is telling you and me? He knew we would come up against Satan's accusations so He made sure we had His promise that He has handled it. Satan has no more control on you or me. God has hurled him down. Satan cannot stand against God. When you feel held down by your past, when the grip of fear and doubt has you in bondage remember that Christ has conquered Satan. You are His and He will strengthen you daily as you seek Him in His Word and through prayer.

I did not have this certainty in my heart overnight. There are still times when a little of that uncertainty tries to hold me in captivity but I now call out to God quickly for His help and He is there immediately reassuring my heart. You and I cannot face each day without Christ. He is our only hope. He is the peace that we seek after. God is able to do all things. He will not leave us comfortless.

In John 14:18 Jesus assures us: I will not leave you as orphans; I will come to you. Our Lord promises to come to us. It doesn't get any better than that!

God reminds each of us that to seek Him we are to look to the rock from which we were cut. That rock is Jesus. He blesses His children. He gives us joy and gladness. We will be thankful and sing to Him. Our Lord is righteous and He is our salvation. His strong arm holds us up and gives us hope. Heaven and earth may pass away but our God never fails.

God is our comfort and our strength. God defends us and helps us in our afflictions.

Nothing is too hard for our Lord. Jesus came to proclaim freedom for the captives.

◆

When Jesus Breaks Our Chains

"When they came to Jesus, they saw the man who had been possessed by the legion of demons, sitting there, dressed and in his right mind..."
Mark 5:15 NIV

Chained, naked, lonely, tomb-dwelling, and demon possessed. As you might imagine from this description it is also a very sad story—at the beginning. If the story had ended there it would leave us feeling hopeless and wondering what would become of the poor guy. But this amazing story only begins in hopelessness. Then, he met Jesus.

Jesus simply spoke and this man was healed. I believe that although this man was possessed there was a part of him that ached for Jesus' touch. There was something stirring deep in his soul that caused him to desire to know the Master and Creator of all mankind. Perhaps there was even a time earlier in his life when he heard about Jesus but turned to sin instead of the Savior.

We are all a little like this man. We are all born in chains of sin, clothed only in shame and definitely not in our right minds! But when we meet Jesus all that changes—or it should.

I certainly know what it's like to live in sin and apart from God. But God is merciful. He also came to me in my misery and broke the chains that held me in bondage to sin. After that I wanted to know Him more. I no longer wanted to live my life enslaved to the devil. I wanted to leave my old life behind to pursue a new life that was pleasing to Him.

I cried out to God and with great compassion He delivered me from my life of sin and misery. He broke my chains of bondage and clothed me in His righteousness. My mind is at peace in Him.

God's power to change lives is immense. That man had been a sinful outcast. Jesus spoke healing and peace into his life.

Only God can work wonders like that. He is able to work in our lives if we allow Him full sway. I am truly thankful for His compassion and His grace to all who seek Him. My prayer is to serve Him the rest of my life and enjoy eternity with Him.

Father, You are so good to us. I want to be bound only by Your love and Your forgiveness. I do not deserve all the kindness You have shown me but I humbly thank You for Your salvation. I was lost in sin and disgrace. Out of Your great love for me You restored me and made me a new creation. You broke the chains that held me in the bondage of sin. Chains I could not break on my own. You have clothed me with Your mercy. I pray I will forever sit at Your precious feet and look upon Your face. Thank you, Father. In Jesus' name I pray.

♦

The World's Biggest Fish Story

"From inside the fish Jonah prayed to the Lord his God."
Jonah 2:1 NIV

It was only when he was in the big fish that Jonah finally cried out to God. Why did he wait so long? Why do *I* call out to God only when I'm in a bad situation?

Could it be a stubborn and rebellious heart? Could I ever be disobedient to God as Jonah was? Yes I can and I have.

Because of Jonah's disobedience, God prepared a large fish to swallow him. From the belly of a stinking fish Jonah, in his hopelessness called out to the God He had blatantly disobeyed.

True, God's plans will be fulfilled with or without us. However, when God tells us to do something for Him, we'd better do it. He does not want to hear our excuses. God was not letting Jonah off the "hook" so easily.

So it was in the fish that Jonah finally turned to God and cried out for help. In verse 7, he says: *"While I was fainting away, I remembered the Lord, and my prayer came to you."* God will get our attention just as He did with Jonah. We may never be swallowed by a fish, but I am certain that many of you are like myself and have been swallowed up by something.

Unfortunately, sometimes we do as Jonah did and run from what God desires for our lives. In this way we willingly deprive ourselves of His abundant blessings by separating ourselves from His will for us.

Then when we cannot run anymore we cry out to Him for help.

Like Jonah, we will never know complete peace outside of God's will for our lives. Perhaps even now you are drowning in a pool of sin, sorrow, and separation.

You may be drifting on a sea of hopelessness and despair. If so, I urge you to cry out to Jesus. He alone can save you from your deepest suffering.

What's keeping you from God's salvation? I urge you to confess it to the Lord, accept His forgiveness and be ready to do whatever He commands. God loves us just as much as He loved Jonah.

Jonah 3:1-3 (NIV) says: *"The Word of the LORD came to Jonah a second time...Jonah obeyed the word of the LORD and went..."* God is merciful isn't He?

We don't always understand what God is asking us to do but we can trust Him to make all things work for His glory. Many people returned to God because of the message God gave Jonah to tell. God is still commanding us to spread His message. How will we react to God's call? God's work will indeed be done with or without our help.

Will we go in boldness and in faith, or will God need to pull us from the depths of our disobedience before we go where He sends us?

♦

Good News in Our Affliction

*"Create in me a pure heart, O God, and renew a
steadfast spirit within me."*
Psalm 51:10 NIV

Jesus speaks to those who are poor in spirit. I have
known material poverty, but spiritual poverty is infinitely
worse. It is colder and more isolating than anything else I
have ever felt. When God pulled back the curtain of my heart
and revealed to me the depths of my sin I became physically
sick. I found no rest at night. I knew no peace in my heart
and my body trembled from the fear of coming into the
presence of a Holy God. Many days I would be face down on
the floor not able to look up, not able to speak. I could only
groan from deep in my soul. Only God could lift me up from
that place of spiritual poverty. And God did lift me up.

In 1 Samuel 2:8 God's word says: "He raises the poor
from the dust and lifts the needy from the ash heap." I love
these words. I am so glad in my heart that God loves me this
much.

He will do the same for anyone who calls upon His name.

One day everyone will fall before God's throne of grace
and confess with their mouth that Jesus is Lord (Romans
10:9). But why wait when you can enjoy the blessings of God
now?

*Oh my God, how wonderful that you do not leave
us in the ashes of our sin and spiritual poverty.
Thank you for your many blessings and your
kindness to us. In Jesus' name I pray.*

♦

God Has Melted My Heart

"As soon as we heard these things, our hearts did melt."
Joshua 2:11 KJV

I. The Harlot Who Trusted God

When Joshua sent two men to spy out the land, God led them to the home of a harlot named Rahab. God had already prepared Rahab's heart to help these men and to play a role in His great plan for His people. A prostitute seems like the most unlikely person for God to use. But God is like that. He is able to see directly into our hearts. If you have a willing and obedient heart, God can and will do marvelous things through you! Rahab had heard stories of how God rescued His people. She tells how God had caused the hearts of men to melt in fear. Joshua 2:11. But she had faith enough to trust God to protect her and her family, if she would serve Him.

She showed courage in hiding these men but it also showed her faith in a God she had only heard about. I pray God will melt our hearts and we will trust Him to not only protect us but to use us for His glory.

II. Hanging by a Thread

"...and she tied the scarlet cord in the window." -Joshua 2:21

The God who Rahab obeyed is the same God of love we obey today. And just as God used Rahab, He can use us.

God instigated a great plan in Jericho for the furtherance of His people. But at the same time, He changed Rahab's life through her willingness to help Him in this plan. Her willingness to obey God would even put her into the lineage of Jesus Christ, the Savior of the world! But all of this hung by a thread—a scarlet cord hanging from Rahab's window.

God uses the small, sometimes seemingly insignificant details for His victory and glory. He, of course, is never limited by what you or I do or don't do. His plans never change. I am amazed at how God can transform the willing heart of a prostitute and a simple scarlet cord to help further the lineage of Christ. Just thinking about everything God did in this story blows my mind! It definitely gives me a renewed hope and reassures me that God is truly a God of love.

I would love to know more about Rahab, how greatly God changed her life and that of her entire family.

Rahab later married an Israelite named Salmon. Matthew 1:5 records that Salmon and Rahab were the parents of Boaz. Boaz married Ruth who gave birth to Obed. Obed would become the father of Jesse who would in turn become the father of King David. Compare these verses to those in Ruth 4:16-22.

What a sweet picture of God's amazing grace. God will forgive, restore, and bless anyone who humbly and sincerely seeks Him. Any one of us can be used by God for His kingdom and His glory.

You are not insignificant to God. You are so precious to Him that He would give His son for you. I am sure that Rahab had no idea how her act of obedience would be rewarded long after her death. God has a plan for each of us. Don't miss your opportunities!

♦

Out of the Darkness

*"The people remained at a distance, while
Moses approached the thick darkness where God was."*
Exodus 20:21 NIV

Moses literally entered darkness for a saving work. He approached a literal, thick darkness where God was in order to save the children of Israel.

At that time a mediator such as Moses was needed between men and God. Now, because of Christ's sacrifice, we can approach His throne of grace anytime in prayer on our own behalf. Even in the most uncertain, darkest times in our life God is there. But He does not leave us where He meets us. He takes us forward! He will draw us ever closer to Himself. Trust Him when you can't see your next step. Cling to Him in that day of affliction and uncertainty. Believe that God is with you always, especially in the dark times of your life. God is near, He hears our cries, our prayers, and He knows our every need.

If your path is dark at this moment in your life, be encouraged. Be assured that God is in the darkness with you. He is all the light we need. Remember these wise words from the Psalmist: *"You, LORD, keep my lamp burning; my God turns my darkness into light."* (Psalm 18:28 NIV); *"Then they cried to the LORD in their trouble, and He saved them from their distress. He brought them out of darkness, the utter darkness, and broke away their chains."* (Psalm 107: 13-14 NIV) Also, *"you have searched me, LORD, and you know me...Where can I go from your Spirit? Even the darkness will not be dark to you..."* (Psalms 139 NIV).

Jesus is our Light. He is the Light of the whole world, a world in darkness. He came to shine light in this darkness. We too must display the Light of God to the world.

We must seek to help those living in sin and darkness. We must show them the way to God. Let us Remember always that *"God is light; in him there is no darkness at all"* (1 John 1:5 NIV).

53

He not only brings into our lives His amazing love and light, He broke the chains that held us there! We are released from the bondage of sin. Our shackles are broken and our darkness turned to light. We are in the presence of our Lord. He is the Light of our lives here on earth and will be our eternal Light in heaven.

♦

I Choose To Be Okay

"...Choose for yourselves this day whom you will serve..."
Joshua 24:15 NIV

A friend who knew about a painful situation facing my family asked me how I was doing.

"I'm okay," I responded. And then I added, "I choose to be okay."

By God's grace alone I can press on. On my own I would be angry, hurt, bitter, and unforgiving. My lack of compassion or love would cause my heart to become hard and cold. My unwillingness to forgive would cause greater separation between me and my Savior. This would all simply add to my misery.

I choose to be okay. I choose to allow God to give me peace of mind and strength of body. This may sound easy. I assure you that it is not. In a moment of human weakness, I may let my guard down, lowering my shield of faith. When that happens I find myself back in the mire of misery again: My joy lost, my peace gone, my outlook dim. I am adversely affected mentally, physically, emotionally and spiritually. I am completely wiped out.

At such times although I may be wiped out spiritually and physically, I find no rest. My heart cannot be at peace apart from God. This is why daily I must choose to be okay. This is why every day I must choose to allow God to take on this burden. Remember that with God all things are possible. Nothing is too hard for Him according to (Jeremiah 32:17 NIV).

God wants us to live close to Him. He wants us to be so close, in fact, that when someone or some situation causes us alarm we will cry out to Him quickly. He will always be there. He has promised that He will never leave or forsake us (Hebrews 13:5 NIV).

Commit to the following every single day:

1) Daily accept that you have absolutely no control over what others say or do. That's in God's hands.

55

2) Daily ask God the Father to touch your heart, soul, and mind so that He may heal you completely.
3) Daily choose the One who has chosen you. Choose God (See 1 Peter 2:9).

Jesus, the son of God, suffered for you and me! By His stripes we are healed (1 Peter 2:24). He not only suffered but died. I know that He died even for those who I personally find so hard to love (Hebrews 2:9-10). Imagine that!

God is daily molding me into a person He can use for His glory. At times the process is slow and painful, but God will ultimately fashion me into a woman who can bring honor to Him (Jeremiah 18:3-6). He can do the same for you. I choose to praise Him for that.

♦

Just a Touch

She only touched the hem of His garment. The glory of Jesus flowed through its very threads. Only the power of Jesus could heal this woman. Only the touch of Jesus could bring the healing she needed. She recognized her need for healing. She had struggled on her own for years. She had searched for healing but had not found it. No one could give her the healing she needed. No one could meet her need. She was tired and lonely. An outcast considered unclean.

Have you ever been there? I'm not talking just spiritually. I'm talking emotionally, physically, mentally, down to nothing, with nothing to lose. Can you see yourself in the place of this woman? Hers was a physical need, but I believe it was a spiritual need as well. By her faith in Jesus she reached out and touched Him. She didn't sit still and just hope she would be healed, she reached out her hand and touched the very robe of Christ!

You are probably saying to yourself, "When will I ever get to see Jesus this side of Heaven?" My dear friend, He sees you wherever you are. Whenever we reach out in prayer our words touch His very heart. He hears our every word even in those times when our heart and soul is so terribly heavy all we can do is utter a groan. Yes, He hears and He is able to heal you. Praise God! Jesus will not leave you broken and in need.

Out of utter desperation this precious, but unclean, woman dared to reach out for Jesus. Immediately she was healed! Immediately Jesus knew she had touched His robe. He knew her heart. He knew her need. He knew she trusted Him enough to reach out to Him. He knows you and me just the same as He knew this woman.

We are all pursuing something. But if Jesus is not the center and foundation of your search you will eventually be back to where this woman was in her greatest need. Only the touch of Jesus will bring healing. She recognized this and did not allow her opportunity to pass by. Will you?

I have asked Jesus into my heart. I have asked for His healing and forgiveness. I know Him and He knows me, but I desire more. I don't want to settle for just a touch of His garment. I want to be wrapped in His cloak of righteousness, completely healed and restored. I pray I never let another opportunity pass me by.

At this time in your life are you weak and hurting? Are you desperate for healing and forgiveness? What prevents you from reaching out to Jesus? You have nothing to lose; you have an eternity of peace to gain.

Push your way past everything in your life that crowds out Jesus. Reach out to Him in prayer this minute. Stop doubting and fall on your face before Him. Allow Him to touch you and make you whole.

This woman went away healed, forgiven and loved. She was made a new woman in Christ. Will you allow Jesus to do the same for you? Don't miss your opportunity.

◆

Our Strength Every Morning

"O Lord, be gracious to us; we long for you. Be our strength every morning, our salvation in time of distress."
Isaiah 33:2 NIV

The year 2010 was a difficult time for our family. It was a dark time for me both emotionally and spiritually. I still cannot write about it without tears coming to my eyes.

Many mornings I would come before the throne of God in prayer searching for relief from the turmoil. Days and weeks would pass with the hurt and bitterness still present. It seemed as if God did not hear my prayers. But I knew in my heart I could trust God to bring good out of this time in our lives. I believed if I could just hang on to God and trust Him through this dark time, He would bring victory. God *has* brought me through and *has* given our family a light at the end of this journey. He is that Light.

I realize now why it seemed so long before God brought relief to my situation. I had failed to place my anger before Him. I sinfully held on to my   resentment for the past actions of another person. Jesus, the Son of God, came to earth to bring release from darkness for the prisoners. Release from my anger and my sin. He came to show each of us that we need God's help to do this. I had been a prisoner, held in bonds by my sinful unwillingness to accept His help.

My spiritual battles still war within me. Daily I have to guard against the evil one's attempts to get me to dwell on the hurt of the past. But daily God renews my strength and sheds His light of compassion into my heart.

My hope is that you will realize we all struggle with our feelings and emotions. But God is alive and real. He is not just an emotion. He is our Creator God and He knows us individually. He does hear our prayers even when we feel like the prayers we pray are falling to the floor. God hears the prayers of those who seek His face.

My prayer is that during your times of darkness and despair you too would call upon the name of the Lord Jesus

Christ. During these times remember passages like Psalm 30:5: *"weeping may remain for a night, but rejoicing comes in the morning."* Sometime our night is not just a few hours! It may be days, weeks or years. But however long our night may be, our rejoicing will come if we patiently wait for it!

Father, I brace myself as I ask you to shine the light of your glory into my heart and reveal any unconfessed sin hidden there. Teach me to be tolerant of others, but not tolerant of their evil ways. Help me to love as you love. I don't want to be involved in schemes or plans of vengeance that may cause me spiritual harm. Give me the grace to love those who hurt me. Forgive my sin that separates me from you. I need and want to be as close to you as I can be at all times. Father, my tears seem to never end. When I think I have moved past the hurt, the evil one floods me with the same bitter thoughts. The anger consumes me. How can I forgive unless you help me God? It has been a long journey, and the night drags on. When will I "rejoice in the morning?" Why do I hold on to feelings that cause me such grief? Why can't I move past this hurt? It seems as if those who bring this hurt don't have a care in the world? If I could see in their heart would they be hurting also? Help me to forgive and to pray for those that cause me and my family this hurt. Father, heal my hurting heart and allow me to rejoice with you. I love you Jesus. You are precious and your mercy is new every morning. By Your grace and strength I can face each new challenge that comes into my life. In Jesus' name I pray.

♦

God's Vengeance

*"To proclaim the year of the LORD's favor, and the day
of vengeance of our God..."*
Isaiah 61:2 NIV

I. Learning Compassion

The word vengeance seems cruel. Yet how many times have I wished I could have vengeance on someone? How often have I prayed with anger and bitterness in my heart? But God in all His mercy has compassion for me and He understands my feelings.

Even as I sit writing these words my vision is blurred by tears of shame and conviction. I am certain I avoided this verse because it would bring me face to face with my own sin; my vengeful, selfish feelings. Such feelings are definitely not of God.

I prayed God would do something about my pain and my family's suffering. God *did* do something. He allowed me to wallow around in my pool of misery and self-pity until I was completely exhausted!

God also showed me something that was wrong in my heart. I had sinfully desired to see the person who caused this pain, feel the same way. This selfish and spiteful desire only created a gulf between me and God.

It also caused many sleepless nights and loss of hair! I was shedding like our dog, Skip!

I got tired, cranky, bitter, and balder. I refused to let go of my pain and anger. Months would pass before I allowed God to bring healing to my heart and soul.

Now my tears are not of sadness, but of overwhelming thanks to God for His mercy and forgiveness. I still have times when I battle those "old feelings of vengeance." It is a constant spiritual battle, but it isn't one I fight alone. God is faithful to supply all the grace I need for that moment.

The vengeance of God against evil is holy because He is holy.

61

And He is so much more. He is also just and compassionate and long suffering. He *could* just wipe us all out because of our sinfulness, but instead He chooses to bestow grace and mercy.

Not only does He give this blessing to me, He absolutely demands that I do the same. Outside of a close relationship to God, it is impossible to live a life of obedience and compassion toward those who hurt us. I am instructed by God to love all people and pray for them—and to really mean it!

II. The Day of God's Vengeance

God will take care of His judgment on His own, in His way and in His own time. We know this because He says so throughout Scripture. The book of Isaiah has some of the best things to say about this (Isaiah 34:8, 35:4, 47:3, 59:17 & 18, and 63:4).

Fortunately, God is not like us. He does not have the same selfish and petty desires. God has been very patient with us throughout history. He has sent men and women to tell of His great love for mankind. He has forgiven me much and continues to forgive me daily. He is not willing that any should perish. He loves everyone.

God is compassionate. He shows mercy even to the vilest of sinners. I know, because I was one. The most amazing gesture of His love for us was when He gave up His only Son so we could have salvation. God is not willing that any should perish, not even the meanest one you or I know. God loves people like that too.

There is a day in God's plan when those who have continued to deny Him will experience His vengeance. Those that profess to love Him yet live their lives outside of His will shall also see His wrath. In the very day of His judgment everyone who has ever lived will stand before the holy God of heaven and earth. There will be no place to hide that He won't uncover. There will be no sin left un-confessed. We will be accountable for what we did or did not do for Christ. Indeed, God's day of vengeance will come.

God forgive me for the times I have failed to witness for you. Forgive me for failing to adequately warn others about Your coming day of judgment. Burden my heart for lost souls. Give me boldness to share the story of Jesus and His love. In Jesus' name I pray.

◆

I Prayed for You

"...Pray for each other so that you may be healed."
James 5:16 NIV

Father, I must confess, that it has been a long time since I could even mention their name in prayer. In my own strength I couldn't, or I just wouldn't let go of the pain. But just today you brought their memory flooding into my mind, and my heart was moved because of their suffering.

Oh, I can remember how not to long ago I was determined to let them go. I could barely look upon their face, but God, you are stronger than my bitterness. Thank you. I praise you for your mercy and your grace.

God only you can move me past this hurt. They have caused so much grief, but I know they need to feel your touch. God, cover them in your hands and calm their fears. I have been there where they are now and it is hard. And it is painfully lonely.

Father, forgiving them goes against all that I want to do. Truly in my heart I desire to be a kind and loving person, just as you are to me. I know I have a long way to go. Now, as I seek your face, I pray for your forgiveness. I have self righteously cast the first stone at them. When in reality we are all sinners. They are no different than me or any one who seeks your love and forgiveness. Their pain is as deep as the hurt they have caused me and others.

In my anger and bitterness, I wanted them to feel the same hurt. But now that they are, I am moved with compassion and I feel the suffering with them. I struggle with the memory of so many sleepless nights, as I watched the one I love cry, not just cry Father, but sob uncontrollably under the weight of rejection. Yet I am moved to pray for this one as they now feel the same pain.

Oh, precious Lord Your compassion wells up within my heart. This can only be from You. I know I am not able to love this deeply on my own.

Father if it is only through these tears that You can cause me to truly love as you do, I pray the tears never cease. Plunge me deeply into your waters of forgiveness and bring me up a woman yielded to your ways.

Amazing God, if I live a thousand more years I will just begin to know the greatness of your love. My mind cannot hold the thought of it, though my heart has been touched by the mercy of it. Please be patient with me a sinner saved only by your amazing and undeserved grace. You are good to us Father...always.

In Jesus' name I pray.

♦

Patient Love

"Love is patient..." 1 Corinthians 13:4 NIV

While looking up the definition of patience I read the following words and phrases: Not easily angered, endurance, calmness, quiet and perseverance. These words definitely do not describe me! Lately I have only shown perseverance in being angry. God has a lot of work yet to be done in my life. The reality is God is able if I am willing. My willingness is the problem! I am not willing to let down my guard to allow God to work in my heart.

I'm not doing very well for a woman who professes to love the Lord. In fact, there are probably lots of people who don't even claim to be Christians who love truer and deeper than I do. My tendency is to do what is necessary to shield my family and myself from the hurt. I certainly don't want to love the one who has caused the hurt. I am thankful God's love is as patient with me as it is with those I find hard to love. I am slowly beginning to allow God to cover my wounds with His healing balm. With His help I will be able to show the same love and forgiveness that He has so graciously shown on me.

God, how can I love the way You command me to? I know I cannot without Your Spirit's love flowing through me. I desire to possess and to share the same love You have for me. It would require that I forgive and be patient with people who seek to cause me trouble.

Throw me some arm floats, Father, because I'm drowning! I had convinced myself that I have forgiven my enemies; You showed me I haven't yet. God, forgive me for not loving as you command me to love.

I am spiritually weak. I will need your strength to let go of this pain. This will not be an easy thing for me, Father. I already anticipate the next confrontation and I feel the hesitation welling up within me. It is very hard to forgive and to love when the one I am required to forgive continues to sow seeds of discontent. But I am no different when I continue to disobey your command to pray for those who hurt me.

I know you pray for me Father. I love you for your mercy and compassion. How I desire to have that same love for others, even when it hurts.

In Jesus' name I pray.

♦

Planted by the Lord

"...The days of your mourning will be over. Then all your people will be righteous; they will possess the land forever, the branch of my planting, the work of my hands, that I may be glorified."
Isaiah 60:20-21 NASB

God has a plan for His children. At this present time you may feel left out and forgotten. Look up! I literally looked up out of my kitchen window. I saw the top of a large oak tree across the road. It stands tall and firm. I considered that big oak tree. When the strong winds rush through the branches, it sways and leaves fly from it. But the oak is strong. It continues to stand firm. The roots are deep in the ground, planting it firmly in place.

The Oak tree is a reminder to stand firm on the promises of the Word of God. There will be times when we experience the winds of life hurling doubts and fears at us. We may bend with the pressure, but we can stand firm in Christ.

This passage reassures us one day there will be no more mourning. For the suffering saint who has known more pain than pleasure: Your day of healing and comfort is coming. To the one who struggles daily with addiction or abuse, God is coming to your rescue. To the one whose heart has been broken by divorce or the death of a loved one, God is bringing wholeness and happiness into your life again. To all who have waited patiently for the Savior's return: You will see Him in all His glory. We will bow at the feet of Jesus, the holy Son of God. The Son of Righteousness, He is our righteous Judge. He is our strong Oak. We are His branches and we will stand firm as a tree planted by our Lord and Savior Jesus Christ.

♦

Amazing Love

"I have loved you with an everlasting love..."
Jeremiah 31:3 NIV

I must admit I do not have the heart of love God wants me to have. Many times I have cried out to God: "I don't want to be a loving person right now! I want to be angry! I'm not ready to love like you love Jesus!"

In my heart I know I must move past my hurt and bitterness. I cannot be the woman God intends for me to be as long as I hold on to these negative and unforgiving feelings.

I know God sees my heart. I know He loves me and understands how I feel. He sees my anger and it hurts Him. He sees my frustration and He understands it. I also know He expects me to roll each of these burdens onto Him and seek Him in prayer for a changed heart.

God has commanded His children to live lives of mercy and grace. Christ has certainly shown me these blessings. He expects no less of me than I extend the same mercy I have been given.

Father, I pray You will forgive my anger, my bitterness, and my unforgiving attitude. Create in me a spirit of love. Help me see even the most unloving person through Your eyes and love them with Your heart. As You change my heart I ask You to also touch the heart of those who threaten to steal my joy and peace.

Father, Your love is more amazing than anything I can ever imagine. I pray I will grow spiritually to be the woman You intend for me to be.

Please empty my heart of all my selfish desires and fill me with Your love.

Father, even as I write these words I find it difficult to let go of the hurt in my heart. I know I cannot be pleasing to

You until I completely surrender my heart to You. I am definitely struggling here. I know You are pleading with me to allow You full sway in my life. Humbly I lay this heavy weight at Your feet.

Precious God of love, please restore my peace and renew my strength. Enable me to walk away from this sin that separates me from You, Father. I must leave it at Your altar of mercy. Only in Your strength can I move forward from this place in my life. Oh, that my heart would beat with the same love You have. God pour Your love into my heart.

In Jesus' name I pray.

♦

Grandchildren

"But from everlasting to everlasting the LORD's love
is with those who fear Him and His righteousness
with their children's children."
Psalm 103:17 NIV

As I watered the flowers late one evening I noticed many brown and bare spots of ground all over the front yard. Above each of these spots was a swing. Our grandchildren spend a lot of time in these swings. Sometimes they will go as high as they can before making a brave jump. At other times they will just sit in the swing while dragging their feet. Sometimes they will twist themselves around and around before letting go. They will twirl around until they are dizzy and laughing. I get nauseated just watching them!

My heart's prayer is that we will enjoy those bare spots left behind by our grandchildren for many more years. And I pray their lives will be lived to serve God. I pray they walk in His ways. I pray they will bring glory to Him.

And may the God of all creation strengthen them and guide them. I pray they grow to be strong and courageous and in love with God.

♦

My Ashes, God's Beauty

"...To bestow on them a crown of beauty instead of ashes...
Isaiah 61:3 NIV

I. A Flower in the Fire

As I walked in the yard one day I passed by an area used for burning brush. My husband frequently has a pile of dead branches to be burned. And the grandchildren love this, because it gives them many opportunities to roast marshmallows and hot dogs.

On this particular day I noticed a tiny sprout coming up out of the ashes of the fire pit. In a way only God can communicate, I was reminded how He brings beauty out of ashes. I have seen this in a very real way in my own life. God has amazingly blessed me, by allowing me to see the beauty in His creation.

Think about it. By His voice alone He created our world and every living creature (Genesis 1). I should not be amazed that He can cause new life to spring forth out of barrenness. He created everything out of nothing! I stand in awe of His power. This small plant peeking out from that burned out ground reminds me of the new life God has given me. Oh my, how He has touched me and made my life beautiful *in* Him. God has brought beauty from the ashes of my past and in Him I am made a new creation. 2 Corinthians 5:17 (NIV) says, *"Therefore, if anyone is in Christ, the new creation has come: The old has gone, the new is here!* I praise Jesus, the Son of God, for His compassion and His salvation. Because of Him each day is a new blessing.

♦

The Veil

*"The curtain will separate the Holy Place
from the Most Holy Place."*
Exodus 26:33 NIV

Pull back the veil that covers my face;
I have come to see God in this place.
Just to gaze at Him and see
God's precious Lamb of Glory.

Pull back the veil.

Calvary was the price He paid;
A borrowed tomb was His grave.
Satan will never again stand;
He'll not defeat God's love for man.

Pull back the veil.

I was that sinner face down and lost
When Jesus cried from that cross:

It is finished!

Oh death, where is your sting?
He closed His eyes in sacrifice,
He has risen to be our King.

God tore the veil!

God is incredibly holy. We must remove our sandals
when we stand before Him for surely we stand on holy
ground. But the veil has been taken away. We do not need a
human priest to go to Him for us. We can now look directly
into His precious eyes. It is finished indeed!

Father, I am humbled and forever thankful for your forgiveness and restoration. I know how unworthy I am. I know that it is only by your grace and love that heaven's doors are flung open wide. There is now no veil to separate me from you. Without your sacrifice, precious Jesus, no one could ever know the glory of heaven. You saw the misery of man. In deep compassion and amazing love you died at Calvary for our salvation. When you breathed that last breath, the veil was forever torn by the holy hands of God the Father. We need never again be separated from You, Our Savior. In Jesus' name I pray.

♦

Brokenhearted

"He has sent me to bind up the broken hearted."
Isaiah 61:1 NASB

Jesus came to bind up the brokenhearted. Is that you? Regardless of what has caused your brokenness, God cares for you. Yes, Jesus came to help those with broken hearts. Are you crushed by grief, spiritually shattered, separated from God and mentally, physically, and emotionally exhausted? If you can answer "yes" to any of these then lift up your head for God has sent you a Savior. His name is Jesus.

Jesus knows what grieves us. He can identify with our pain because he experienced it in a number of ways. He experienced physical pain in suffering and dying at Calvary. He experienced emotional pain. John 11:35 says that Jesus wept. In that passage, He was grieving and mourning the death of His friend Lazarus. He experienced despair and brokenness. Luke 19:14 says, *"As He (Jesus) approached Jerusalem and saw the city, He wept over it."* Why was Jesus crying for Jerusalem? Verse 44 says that it was *"Because they did not recognize the time of God's coming."*

Jesus was brokenhearted that His own people did not recognize who He was. Before we are quick to throw our self-righteous stones at them let us take a quick look at ourselves. You're probably thinking "well, they could see Jesus with their eyes and we haven't even seen Him at all." But remember we walk by faith not by sight (2 Corinthians 5:7).

Jesus shed tears for Jerusalem. He sheds tears for us today. Yes, He weeps over and prays for us in continuous intercession. In other words, He is our "go-between."

Romans 8:34 says that *"Christ Jesus, who died, more than that was raised to life, is at the right hand of God and is also interceding for us."*

Jesus came to bind up every broken heart. Will you let Him bind yours?

Father, you search our hearts and you know our brokenness. I pray for those who at this moment feel isolated, forsaken, and brokenhearted. They need your comfort and peace. Jesus, touch those precious souls who are lost and still in need of You. Bind their hearts to yours so they can have restoration and healing.

Thank you, Father. In Jesus' name I pray.

♦

Faint Not

"But those who hope in the Lord will renew their strength. They will soar on wings like eagles; they will run and not grow weary, they will walk and not be faint."
Isaiah 40:31 NIV

I am trying to teach my grandson that we must fully rely on God, that we must constantly draw a little deeper from the Lord's strength spiritually, physically and emotionally. I bought him a prayer coin that had this verse from Isaiah on it. I wanted him to have something he could look at each day and know I was "rooting" him on. Every time he reached into his pocket he would feel the coin and be reminded of two very important facts: 1) I was cheering him on and 2) God was too and would give him the spiritual strength he needed.

I encourage you to praise God daily and draw from the bottomless well of His strength. If it has never been your habit to praise God, start now by praising Him in small ways. Make it a point to praise Him every day, all day. When your strength fails and you feel you cannot go on, ask God who gives you the strength you need to endure.

When your load seems too heavy to bear, call on the One who can and will keep you from fainting. There are days I feel I cannot go another step. I get discouraged when I forget that; through Jesus Christ I am able to do all I need to do. He gives me my strength.

Faint not, dear child of the King. Your hope is in Him. You are strong in the Lord. He will cause your heart to soar and renew your spirit. We will run our race and not be weary. We will walk with Him and He will not allow us to faint. Praise Him!

♦

Comfort for the Mourning

"To proclaim the favorable year of our lord...to comfort all who mourn."
Isaiah 61:2 NASB

One morning I read Nehemiah 9 during my personal devotion. A certain phrase in the verse caught my eye: *"Because of our sins....we are in great distress."*

I did not have peace and I was struggling. I had not been as close to the Lord as I should; I was feeling the separation. God had not abandoned me; I had abandoned Him. I had allowed too many things to make me busy. Consequently, my time with the Lord was at a minimum. I was beginning to feel the effects.

In Isaiah 61 we are told that God will comfort all who mourn. When I think of mourning, death is the first thing that comes to mind. But I was experiencing a type of mourning that did not result from a physical death. I was suffering because I was neglecting my time with God. I had not been to Jesus in a few days for a spiritual "fill-up" and I could tell it in my heart and mind.

Because of my sin of disobedience and self-reliance I was, in a sense, "mourning" a broken relationship. For me it was a silent, withdrawn, absence of joy in my heart and soul, kind of mourning. God is good in that He does not allow me to wander too far before He sends His spirit to touch my heart and convict me of my sin. We must never believe that we have been so long with the Lord that we can neglect Him whenever we want. We must daily spend time with the Father who created us. We are created to glorify Him. How can you or I do that if we don't even have a personal relationship with Him?

The evil one is subtle in drawing each of us away from Jesus. Then in a spiritual sense we experience mourning. Draw near to God who draws near to you.

So that day as I read that passage in Nehemiah, I sat there at my kitchen table and bowed my head in prayer.

What a day that turned out to be! It happened to be Easter Sunday, the day we celebrate the resurrection of Jesus!

I know our Father loves us deeply. When we choose not to spend time with Him, it grieves Him. He misses our time together. Jesus mourns our absence. But I am humbled and thankful to know that He forgives us and continues to bring comfort to those of us who mourn.

♦

My Example Matters to God

"For what will it profit a man if he gains the whole world and forfeits his soul? What will a man give in exchange for his soul?"
Matthew 16:26 NASB

Our grandson's passion is baseball. Since he was in diapers he has been on the ball field. Back then he watched from the bleachers with us as we cheered on his uncle. Today he plays at the same high school. I have *always* enjoyed watching their games. One particular night the coach pulled our grandson out of the game. Was he hurt? What happened that would cause him to be removed from the game? We found out later that he had used profanity. I respect the coaches for their discipline but I was so disappointed in our grandson's actions.

My grandson's behavior got me to thinking. I know I have been guilty of saying things I shouldn't say so why was I holding him at a higher level of accountability? I shouldn't—that's the point. We each paint a portrait of who we are by our actions, words, and deeds. In baseball terms, I have struck out far more times than I have hit homeruns!

I'll continue with the baseball analogy. In baseball hitting a homerun is every player's dream. This is especially true in high school. It doesn't get any better, right?

Well, it does get better. Hitting a homerun in real life and finishing up at home in eternity--that's a grand slam!

Who gives man the ability to think or speak or do anything? God! He alone is the Creator of all. He gives gifts and abilities to each of us. How we use them and the example we set while using them is a reflection on God, on family and ourselves. We are created to glorify God whether it is hitting a baseball over the centerfield fence or simply holding a friend's hand in times of discouragement or grief. All we do should be done for God's glory.

♦

Oil of Gladness

"Gladness and joy will overtake them, and sorrow
and sighing will flee away."
Isaiah 35:10 NIV

In Luke 7 we can read the moving story of a sinful woman seeking God's forgiveness. She knew of her great need for the Savior's touch. She came to Jesus, bringing with her an expensive bottle of perfume and tears streaming down her cheeks. She bathed His feet with fragrant perfume mingled with her tears of repentance and dried them with her hair. She knew all too well what it was like to be held in the grip of sin. She also knew that the only one who could release that hold was Jesus.

Others may have tried to find fault in her actions, but not our Savior. He had deep compassion for her. He has that same compassion for us.

Oh how I can see myself in this woman. I too have been forgiven much. Our sins may differ but the scars left behind are just as real. God has rescued me from the deep waters of sin and set me on the shore of His mercy. Still, I have wandered back many times, drawn to the very sinful life from which He saved me. But He has never failed to grant me forgiveness when I have sought Him with a broken heart pleading for His grace. He is always there patiently waiting, with arms outstretched. With a heart of infinite love, He restores my gladness. His grace is the oil of gladness He pours over me.

You may be thinking "that's me, I have sinned greatly and I desperately want to be forgiven." Just come as you are to the feet of Jesus. All you need to do is ask Him to cleanse you of the filth that sin has left in your life. I pray you do so right now.

He will *always* be faithful to heal our hearts and restore our gladness. The tears that flowed from this woman's eyes onto the holy feet of our Savior continue to remind us we too have been forgiven much by our infinitely forgiving Lord.

The Rains Will Come

"Let my teaching fall like rain and my words descend like dew..."
Deuteronomy 32:2 NIV

It's a rain-out. Who hasn't witnessed one of these at a ball game? As I mentioned, we have spent many hours on the ball field with our son and grandsons. Not often, but occasionally the game will be delayed or cancelled due to a rain-out.

As I thought on this, it occurred to me how we all have unexpected rain-outs during our lives. This was made real to me when my family and I endured a severe storm that momentarily shook us but did not carry us away from the protective arms of Jesus.

Rain did come into our lives. It came swiftly and without notice. When this happened we huddled together to protect each other from the storm. This "rain-out" continued for at least a year. Even now we continue to have pop-up showers that are the remnants of that big storm.

These unexpected storms that pop-up often start small, but if left unattended they too can develop into dangerous conditions in our walk with the Lord. They bring clouds of fear and doubt, anger, bitterness and suspicion. I shamefully admit that I felt each of these during our recent storm. I still pray daily for God to deliver me from their lingering effects.

We were never alone, as a family we had each other, but greater still we had God. He covers us during the pop-up storms, shielding us from the "rain drops" of adversity. At times the rain was so harsh it almost washed us out physically and certainly caused devastating emotional grief. In the darkest moment God responded to the groan of our hearts. He lifted us up and provided the shelter and strength we needed at just the right time.

As a coach hurries to cover the field to protect it from the rain, so our Lord ran to us and covered us with His cloak of righteousness.

He does this because we are His handiwork, created for His glory. With love and intricate detail He made us. With those same hands He will protect us from the rains that threaten us.

No, God did not prevent the rain from coming into our lives. I admit I often asked why. But God assured me we were never alone. Through it all God drew us near to Him and helped us to know we could trust Him through this storm. By His grace and mercy we remained strong.

Right now while I am writing, the sun is shining. But I must remember that rain-outs can come quickly and without notice.

I do not enjoy the rain-outs but I cherish the showers of blessing God brings to all who seek Him and love Him. If I never had the rain I would possibly take for granted the brightness and warmth of God's Son. How blessed we are to have Him in our hearts and lives.

I love you Lord for being the anchor of my family. You are so good to us. We are truly blessed. Thank you for covering us and giving us strength in our times of uncertainty. In Jesus' name I pray.

♦

In God

*"The power of the LORD came on Elijah; and tucking his cloak
into his belt he ran....*
1 Kings 18:46 NIV

The God that gave Elijah his strength and ability is the same God who still gives strength and ability to His servants. Yes, He is *your* God and He is *my* God. *Our* God is the only true, living God. He is the same yesterday, today, tomorrow and all eternity.

Our verse says that Elijah girded himself, and got up and ran. Likewise we must also get up and run the race before us. God will enable us to do this. It may not be an easy path, but God will bring us through our valley of discouragement. Just as He was with Elijah He is with us.

Yes, we will surely encounter difficulties along our journey. We will experience periods of physical and emotional weakness. That is one reason why we must gird ourselves up and run to Jesus. We must cling to the One who keeps us safely in His hands. We must keep our hearts and eyes fixed on the One who has His eyes on us.

◆

Waves of Doubt

*"...The one who doubts is like a wave of the sea blown
and tossed by the wind."*
James 1:6 NIV

The first time I visited the beach it had not been too long after a hurricane. The water was so rough that red flags were posted to warn visitors of the hazardous conditions. When we were able to get into the ocean the water continued to be so chaotic that at times we were knocked off our feet. I know this because I am a survivor of this post hurricane experience! One minute I'm enjoying life and laughing with my family, the next I'm sitting on the ocean floor, feet over my head (not a pretty sight!), and struggling to resurface! Approximately three waves and two lungs filled with salt water later, I emerged from the watery depths. I can almost relate to Jonah— except a big fish didn't swallow me! I am thankful I had my grandson close by to grab hold of me when I needed help.

Although this was a funny and memorable experience I am able to relate it to other times in my life I have been hit by waves of a different kind. These waves are far from pleasant. They are waves of doubt or fear that try—and sometimes succeed—in knocking me off my spiritual feet and leave me struggling to regain my balance. God knew we would all have experiences like this. But He does not intend for us to face the waves of life alone or without an anchor to hold to. He is our anchor in life's storms. When the storms of life rage—and they will, we can rest secure in the peaceful waters that surround Jesus.

The red flags we saw that day were signals for us to use caution when entering the water. God's Word is used for our instruction and to keep us safe when the waves of life hit hard. Prayer helps us to recognize these red flags also. I am not always faithful to pray. I find myself struggling to keep my feet firmly planted.

God has always been patient, kind, loving, and protective of me. I can't begin to imagine why He loves me so much, but I am humbled and grateful that He does. He loves you the same way. His love is deeper than the ocean and stronger than the stormy waves that roll over us in our times of doubt and weakness.

I laugh every time I am reminded of that beach trip! And I am amazed every time I think about Jesus and His great love for us. His hand has never failed to hold me when I have reached out for Him. No one floats in calm waters *all* the time. You and I will face rough waters. But we do not need to face them alone. God is near to all who call on His name. Let Him be your strength and your anchor in life's storms.

Jesus I praise you because you are the quiet place I can run to in all life's storms. You speak and the waves are held back and the winds are hushed. You are Creator God and I am humbled at the very thought of you. I was drowning in my sin, but you lifted me up when I cried out to you. I pray for those who are struggling at this moment. As life's turbulent waters rise and the waves cover them, I pray they will call out to the only one who can save them. You rescue those who cry out to you in faith. You are the anchor who holds us securely. Thank you Father. In Jesus' name I pray.

♦

You Had to Be There

"Satan went out from the presence of the LORD and afflicted Job with painful sores from the soles of his feet to the crown of his head."
Job 2:7 NIV

I. Lifted Up

Nothing comes into our lives without God's knowledge. We may drink from the bitter cup of affliction or find rest at His peaceful oasis. You can be certain God carries you through your struggles and cherishes the joyful times with you as well. Although Job experienced great pain and loss, he accepted it and reminded his wife also in verse 10: "...shall we indeed accept good from God and not accept adversity?" He trusted God when his pain was great and rejoiced in Him when God's blessings flowed.

When you are in pain, you want to talk to someone who understands your suffering. When no one else seems to understand, God does.

You do not need to suffer alone. God sees and knows every hurt and need that you have. He will not leave you to face your pain on your own. He will indeed lift you out of your suffering if you will allow Him, or He will give you peace and strength as you go through it.

Perhaps you are currently experiencing pain. What is it that is causing your heartache right now? It may be the intense, unimaginable pain of losing a child. Is it the loneliness of divorce? Is it feelings of failure and worthlessness? Are you, a spouse, or child struggling with an addiction? Have you lost your job, your home, your savings, and with it, your confidence?

You may feel completely alone, misunderstood and unloved. Maybe you are experiencing great physical affliction that has been ongoing and you cry out in your heart: Why Lord? When will my suffering end?

Please trust God, He knows and cares about your suffering. You are not alone.

Even Job who avoided all evil and loved God with his whole heart, found himself sitting in ashes of grief. Job mourned the loss of his children and his body ached for relief from his physical pain. Job's pain was so intense he could not rest. Job chapter 30:17 NIV says: "Night pierces my bones my gnawing pains never rest." Pain will wear you out! His suffering had come upon him suddenly and without warning.

Later in verse 21, of this same chapter, Job cries out to God in his anguish: "You have become cruel to me". Have you ever felt that God was cruel to you? I can assure you God is not cruel.

God is grieved in His heart when we believe such things. But He is ready and willing to forgive the repentant one.

Job reminds God (Who needs no reminding) in verse 25; "Have I not wept for the one whose life is hard? Was not my soul grieved for the needy?" Job remembered the times he helped others. He had cried over them and comforted them. He longed for that same comfort. Not only his body but his soul ached for the comforting touch of God.

God was with Job, the long days he sat in the ashes of his devastation and affliction God never took His eyes off of him.

Job's physical suffering had lingered for so long. Although he may not have realized it, as he went through this valley of suffering, his faith in God, although shaken, was what gave him the strength to endure.

Later in chapter 42:5 NIV Job cries out: "My ears had heard of You; but now my eyes have seen You. In verse 6 Job's ashes of mourning became ashes of repentance.

Job did struggle, but he remained true to God. At the end of his time of affliction God restored Job and blessed his life more than before his suffering.

You must read the book of Job. There is much more that I didn't touch on and it is an amazing testimony to the greatness and loving compassion of our God.

Father, you are the God of our lives.
You are our Comforter.
You are our Great Physician.
You are our Joy.
You are our Strength.
You bring Healing.
You are forgiving.
You Restore our Souls.
You are God.
Thank you.

♦

She Cries

*"Weeping may stay for the night, but rejoicing
comes in the morning."*
Psalm 30:5 NIV

I have experienced the loss of loved ones in my life. I remember when my grandparents passed away. My sister and I were at dad's bedside when he passed away. Although I have experienced this, I cannot begin to know—nor do I ever want to know—the agony of losing a child.

This is a journey a dear friend of mine has traveled. She and her husband know all too well the deep loneliness and suffering that comes from this. They know their precious son is with the Lord and they will one day be reunited. Until then, the two of them are committed to trusting God. They know that He will never allow more in their lives than they can bear.

I was with my sweet friend the night her son died. We sat side by side holding hands. We spent time sharing memories and praying together. But as much as I love her, I cannot begin to know the depths of her pain and brokenness. Fortunately, God does.

Daily thoughts of him must flood her heart and mind and I know she misses him greatly. But I also know that her strength and hope is in the Lord. She trusts in God to see her and her family through this difficult journey. In His great love and compassion, God receives into His comforting arms His grieving children. He will be true to hold them close until they are strong enough to stand again.

I do not understand everything that comes into our lives. It is not meant for us to know everything. We need only trust that God understands all things.

In our suffering it is God's desire that we draw closer to Him, unite or hearts to His, and find rest beneath His wings of grace and mercy.

Thank you, Father, that you do know our pain. Your Son died on a cruel cross so we can have the assurance of eternity in heaven. You, Father, bind up the brokenhearted and bring comfort to the hurting. You are our strength in our weakest moments. You are loving and compassionate. In time, healing will come to those whose trust is in you. In Jesus' name I pray.

◆

Strong in Your Struggle

"But He knows the way that I take; when He has tested me, I will come forth as gold."
Job 23:10 NIV

I. Our Cocoon of Struggle

You have probably heard the story of the butterfly.

The caterpillar wraps itself in a tight cocoon. In the process of time it emerges a beautiful butterfly. It is through the struggle to re-emerge from the cocoon the butterfly develops its strength and beauty. To help or hurry this process would interfere with God's intricate plan for this creature. We are more precious than this lovely butterfly. But we do face struggles. During our difficult times, if we will allow God to work in and through us, we can emerge strong in the Lord and exhibit His beauty.

As I sat in the kitchen enjoying the quiet of the early morning, I prayed for my family. As I prayed, my heart became heavy over the struggles that they were each facing. Spiritual, personal, emotional, financial problems, we all deal with them. They are "every day life" kinds of things that can weigh us down. Still my heart aches to see my family struggle.

God knows every detail. I know He will bring them through. He will give them grace to endure and accept their trials or provide the relief they need from them.

I love my family dearly. It is hard for me to resist the desire to peel them from their cocoon of struggle. I must trust God to give them the strength they need to emerge on their own. They will not gain their spiritual grit and godly beauty, if I do not allow them this time of growth in the Lord.

God has never failed me. I pray I will never fail to lift up my loved ones to Him. God knows our every struggle. He will always be true to enable us to endure. We are His creation, the work of His hands. When our struggles come—and they will— we must trust God. Allow Him to peel back the layers of our cocoon at His leisure.

God has a plan and a purpose for us. But living life for God is definitely not for wimps! It may require a time of struggle to bring out our inner beauty and spiritual strength. We can gain this strength daily from God's Word and through prayer. Little by little, one layer after another will be pulled away from the cocoon that surrounds us. Before we know it, we will emerge beautiful creations of the Lord, created to praise, glorify and worship Him.

> *I trust you, Father, to hold my family in your mighty but gentle hands until their time of struggle has ended. My prayer is to see them walk in beauty and strength because of your wonderful love and grace. I praise You, God of all creation. In Jesus' name I pray*

♦

Who Can Wash Away My Sin?

"Cleans me with hyssop, and I will be clean; wash me,
and I will be whiter than snow."
Psalm 51:7 NIV

We each have our clumsy times. Maybe today you spilled something on your favorite shirt. Or you find a stain on that new dress. I imagine you immediately grabbed your trusty bottle of stain remover and commenced aggressively trying to remove the stain. Sometimes, though, stains are so tough that you can scrub until your knuckles are raw and that stain will not come out. Frustrating! Yet, unwilling to cry "Uncle!" you toss it into the washing machine for one last attempt. But as you pull it out at the end of the cycle, it is apparent that the stain has defeated you once again.

Our lives also have stains like that. We have stains that have settled into the deepest threads of our being. That stain in your life may be an un-confessed sin. We often attempt to rid ourselves of these stains by our own power. Of course, we always fail. But there is someone so amazing and able who is very willing to cleanse every stain.

We may call our stains bad habits or addictions, but understand what they really are—SIN. Try as we might, we cannot rid ourselves of this sin on our own. We must place our sins in God's hands for His cleansing. We can soak all day in a bubble bath, scrub until our fingers are red, but nothing we do can remove the sin staining our hearts and souls. It is only by the cleansing touch of Jesus that we are made completely spotless and thoroughly clean.

Jesus did the hard work for us. When he died on the cross His precious blood flowed to cover our sins and transgressions. No more sacrifice is needed. Just one drop of His life-changing blood can cover a multitude of sin and despair. Praise God!

When Jesus cleanses us, there is no need for us to presoak, super wash, or repeat wash. He came to give life, eternal life, a life free of stains and freely offered to all who will receive Him. Why are you waiting to be cleansed by Jesus? You can do so right now. Acts 22:16 NIV says, *"And now what are you waiting for? Get up, be baptized and wash your sins away, calling on his name."* Our Redeemer has a name and His name is Jesus. But in order to receive this redemption, you must first call out in faith. He will wash the dirtiest sinner clean. I am living testimony of that!

If you call on Him, He will cleanse you of your sin-stained life. Allow Him to bathe you in His love. Let Him plunge you beneath his life-giving blood. Jesus, our Savior, the sinless Lamb of Glory is waiting to make you clean.

◆

Clothed in Praise

"It is good to praise the LORD."
Psalm 92:1 NIV

We are created to praise and glorify God. Our praises are sweet to His ears. He delights in our praise and worship. He desires to hear from His children. Don't we who are parents cherish the voices of our children? It is not hard to imagine that our own heavenly Father also smiles with delight when He hears our voice.

I have been a nurse for many years. I have had the opportunity to meet a lot of people.

I once took care of a precious lady who I'm convinced God brought into my life. Every time she spoke of anything she would follow with: "Praise the Lord!" After our conversation had continued for some time I told her, "It is good to hear you praise the Lord for everything."

She admitted she had not realized how often she said it. Then she began telling me how good God has been to her. She spoke of her "wonderful" husband who in her words "took care of me." He was not a pushy or controlling man. His greatest desire was to be the one to take care of me, and "I let him" she said. What a Christ-like example for all of us. God wants to take care of us like that. He is not pushy or controlling, but rather, loving and providing.

She continued to tell the story of her life with her husband. When her husband became ill, she described how inadequate she felt to take care for him. She felt horrible because her husband had always provided for her needs and she didn't know if she would be able to do the same for him. But then with a big smile of satisfaction she told me, "God gave me the ability to do it and I did it and I am grateful."

Picture this beautiful love story unfolding in Christian language. Jesus has this same kind of love for us. He gives us the ability to do the things we don't believe we have the strength to do. Jesus is the Author of our love story. He is the reason we always have something to sing praises about.

This precious woman also told me about her love for her children. She described how special each one was to her. She joked that none of them even knew her true age! I asked her if she thought they could figure it out. She replied: Yes, they probably could, but they are too sweet to tell me! We both laughed.

Later, when her daughter came in to see her mother she leaned over and gently kissed her on the cheek. It was clear that the relationship between mother and daughter was tight knit. It touched my heart to see their closeness. I spoke to the daughter and commented on her tenderness to her mom. Without any hesitation she said it was because her mother has always shown kindness to me.

In my years as a nurse, I have witnessed many, sweet moments. This was among the sweetest. I mentioned to this dear mother that I was writing this book. I told her I hoped to share their story. I believe God provided this opportunity to share this beautiful story of praise. Here was a woman, whose love for God was so overflowing that it spilled out into the lives of her family. We can have this same testimony. We may not have a lot to offer, but we can all offer praise to God and kindness to our families. Let us daily lift our voices in praise to our Lord and Savior. I know He will pour out His blessings on us and our families too.

◆

We Have Forgotten God

*"The ox knows its master... my
people do not understand."*
Isaiah 1:3 NIV

The Ox Knows.

What a sad pictures this verse brings to mind. Think about it: Even a simple ox knows its master, he knows what he is expected to do, yet we do not recognize our God.

God is our hope and our strength. He knows us and we know Him. But we are prone to wander and to neglect Him. God forgive us. The breath of the One who gave our soul life fills our lungs yet we do not use our voices to praise Him. We do not speak of Him. God how many times are we guilty of placing other unworthy things first in our lives and serving you from a distance? What a shame God's most cherished creations choose not to remember the God who created them.

Yes, even an Ox knows his master. Our Master is Creator and Savior of the world, yet we so often choose not to know Him. How sad indeed.

Father, please hear my humble prayer. Forgive our sins and draw us unto you. Keep us in the protection of your strong arms. As the ox pulls the plow through the hard ground, I pray Your Spirit will till the hard soil of our hearts. Prepare it for the seed of Your Word. I pray that your people today will cry out to you and desire to know You more. Forgive us of our sins, Lord. Gather us as a harvest is gathered into the safety of your shelter. Father, I pray that each of us, your children, will desire to humble ourselves, pray and seek your face. Break our hearts for you Lord and help us turn from our wicked ways. You have promised to always forgive our sin and to heal the land of those who turn to you (2 Chron. 7:14). Thank you for your mercy toward us. In Jesus' name I pray.

Sweetly Spoken

"...show me your face let me hear your voice; for your voice is sweet and your face is lovely."
Song of Songs 2:14 NIV

I was hurt by his words. Words leave scars. My heart ached and I was terribly discouraged. What my husband thinks is important to me. I want him to be able to trust my judgment and have confidence in my decisions. When he doesn't, I am deeply hurt.

My husband and I have been married for over thirty-five years, but we are continuing to grow and change as individuals. We are faced with the challenge of acknowledging those changes and making them work for us as a couple.

After the apologies and hugs of forgiveness, I read the love story found in Song of Solomon. This brought to mind the two most important relationships in my life: my relationship to Christ and my relationship to my husband.

I have prayed for just a glimpse of my Savior's face and to hear His sweet voice speak to my heart. I believe God wants our marriages to be like that as well: Anticipating our time together, sharing sweet conversation, speaking in love and being compassionate with one another.

When my husband shows kindness to me and speaks to me in a loving way, I'm eager and willing to do special things for him. Our home should be a place of comfort and peace, warm, loving and secure. Our relationship to Christ should be the same, because He *is* our comfort (2 Cor. 1:4) and our peace that passes all understanding (Phil. 4:7).

I want to look in my husband's face and hear Him speak sweetly to me. I pray I will remember this verse the next time I get upset. I pray that God will make me a lovely woman with a sweet voice. My husband deserves that kindness from me. I trust God to help me. I know He will.

◆

Year of the Lord's Favor

"The Spirit of the Lord is upon me, because he hath anointed me to Preach the gospel...to preach the acceptable year of the Lord"
Luke 4:18-21 KJV

I. The Lord Has Come

In this passage, Jesus is referring to the mention of the year of the Lord's favor in Isaiah 61:2. A couple verses later in Luke 4:21, Jesus reminds us: *"Today this Scripture is fulfilled in your hearing."* The year of the Lord's favor had come. Jesus came to preach good news to the poor.

He came to be our Great Physician, to bind up the brokenhearted. He has healed my heart. He came to be our liberator from slavery to sin. He has freed me from the captivity of my past through Jesus Christ my Lord and Savior. Jesus brings release from darkness. My darkness has therefore been turned into light. In Him there is no darkness at all. He is the light of the world!

II. Now is the Time!

God knew all too well our desperate need of being saved. He also knew that there was only one way to save us. In His infinite compassion He sent us our Savior, our Lord. He gave the gift of His own Son to be the sacrifice of our sins. Yep, someone else had to die to pay the penalty. And it wasn't just anyone—it was God's son Jesus.

Because of Jesus we now have full access to the eternal benefits of this gift.

Now is the time!

Jesus has already delivered us from whatever holds us in bondage. Jesus, who knew no sin brought to us the grace and forgiveness of God the Father. Only by calling on Jesus' name can you and I be saved from eternal torment in hell. Revelation 14:11-12 records the horrors of this real place: *"And the smoke of their torment rises forever and ever.*

There is no rest day or night." Jesus came to save us from this. By Him we can choose to have eternal life with God. Over and over we read in Scripture how Jesus brought forgiveness, hope, healing, and salvation to all who receive Him. In our world of so much pain and regret, isn't it wonderful to know that Jesus cares about you? Isn't it reassuring to know that nothing can separate us from the love of Christ? Romans 8:35-39 perfectly expresses our victory in Christ:

"Who shall separate us from the love of Christ? Shall tribulation, or distress, or persecution, or famine, or nakedness, or peril or sword? As it is written, for thy sake we are killed all the day long; we are accounted as sheep for the slaughter. Nay, as all these things, we are more than conquerors through Him who loved us. For I am persuaded, that neither death, nor life, nor angels, nor principalities, nor powers, nor things present, nor things to come, nor height, nor depth, nor any other creature, shall be able to separate us from the love of God, which is in Christ Jesus our Lord."

Rejoice!
The time of Jesus' redemption has come.
This is indeed the year of the Lord's favor!

◆

Pieces

"For all have sinned and come short of the glory of God."
Romans 3:23 KJV

Think back to when you were a child. You had that favorite toy, the one thing you held on to every day. You played with it until the paint was faded and the material worn. Maybe a wheel came off the toy truck so you no longer could roll it on your road of wooden blocks. Maybe the arm fell off your favorite doll or the stuffing came out of your favorite stuffed animal. Even worse, maybe your favorite toy was lost. You and your family looked everywhere, but the toy could not be found. Remember the disappointment? Remember the tears?

Sometimes dad could fix what was broken. Sometimes he could not. The lost toy that was never found was eventually replaced by something new. The broken toy that could not be repaired was set on a shelf to be kept and remembered while it collected dust.

This reminds me of my life when I came to Jesus. All I had to offer were broken pieces.

I will never forget the broken pieces I laid on His altar. So much sin and hurt and fear that held me captive. I didn't feel worthy to even ask Jesus to forgive me or even expect Him to actually do so.

But He did! Praise God, He did!

Jesus can bind the wounds and fit all the pieces together again. By the touch of His hand or the whisper of His voice, He repairs broken hearts and brings peace to suffering souls. He will never discard us or place us on a shelf to be of no use. Jesus takes all of our broken pieces and makes us whole. He has done this in my life. He will do it in your life as well when you come to Him seeking forgiveness and restoration. He is a master at making all things new again.

Jesus died on the cross for *all* of our sins. God's Word says we have *all* sinned (Romans 3:23). That includes you and me. Jesus conquered death by not remaining in the

102

grave. In three days He rose from the dead winning the victory over death and hell. His blood shed on the cross has covered our sins. The heavens above and the earth below cannot contain Him. He is truly our awesome God!

My heart is full at this moment just writing about Jesus' great goodness. Because of Him I have been forgiven and I will stand before Him "whole." My sins that were many have been forgiven and forgotten. Maybe you have pieces of your life that need the Master's touch. Right there in your living room while you're crying tears of bitterness just speak His name. Let Him restore you into the beautiful creation He intended you to be. There are no rejects with Christ; He loves us all. He accepts us just as we are then He transforms our lives in ways we can't imagine.

♦

Bees and Honey

"...Never will I leave you; never will I forsake you."
Hebrews 13:5 NIV

I was sitting at my desk praying silently over God's direction in my life.

I suppose that's what people do as they get a little older! I was trying to decide how to approach this devotion. I wanted to write a devotion that would show how something may be painful yet result in something sweet and good. Several options came to mind. I decided to talk about bees. Yes, bees.

Have you ever been stung by a one? Very painful! Yet honey bees produce honey. Very sweet and good! It is the same with me and my relationship to God. God created all of mankind in His image. He *is* love and compassion and forgiveness. Like honey, He is good and sweet. I on the other hand choose at times to be unloving and unforgiving. This is painful not only for God, but for me personally. By my disobedience to Him I lose out on God's peace and joy for my life. This spills over into my family relationships, my friends, and most importantly my spiritual life. If I am not walking in obedience to Christ then I am against Him. And that is not where I want to be!

I am a child of God. I know that God is good and He never leaves me nor forsakes me. He assures me of this in this passage. God's promises are true and lasting. Joshua 23:14 (NKJV) says, *"Behold, this day I am going the way of all the earth. And you know in all your hearts and in all your souls that not one thing has failed of all the <u>good things</u> which God promised you."* Every promise has been fulfilled; not one has failed. To put it simply, this is very good!

God's promises remain real and alive today for those who call upon the name of the Lord in faith. Time after time it is recorded in the Bible how the Israelites strayed away from God. Out of His deep love for them He would receive them back into His arms. Nothing has changed. That is why it is said God's Word is alive. His Word is as true and faithful today as it was those many years ago.

God's Word also says in Psalm 19: 9 & 10 (NKJV), "...*the judgments of the Lord are true and righteous altogether. More to be desired are they than gold, yea, than much pure gold; <u>sweeter also than honey and the honeycomb</u>.*" This is also very, very good!

I am amazed how God, who knows our thoughts, can use them to teach us of His goodness. God can take the sting out of all our hurts when we feast on the nectar of His Word. God is good and worthy of all praise. He is sweeter than honey from out of the comb!

♦

Rejoice

"...we also glory in our sufferings, because we know
that suffering produces perseverance."
Romans 5:3 NIV

Rejoice *always*! That means more than just when times
are good and we feel like rejoicing. God wants us to rejoice
when things are not good (read Philippians 4:4)

It is very hard to rejoice when:

1) Things aren't right with your spouse.
2) Your children are sick, hurt, or spiritually suffering.
3) Your job is miserable and makes you miserable.
4) Your health is failing.
5) You feel like everything is going good then life takes
   an unexpected turn.
6) Your husband's job has ended.
7) You try so hard to make ends meet and everything
   increases except your income.
8) You have prayed for years about something or
   someone without visible results.
9) You're struggling, tired, afraid, hurting, depressed,
   and angry.
10) You're not close to God.

God wants us to be gentle about our frustrations. Let your
gentleness be evident to all (Phil. 4:5).

Yes, rejoice in the Lord <u>and</u> be gentle! That's what God
commands...Is He kidding! How can we rejoice and show
gentleness *all* of the time? My friend, God does not kid
around about being kind and gentle. And He will know. The
rest of that verse says, "*The Lord is near.*" If the Lord says
He is near, then He will know our actions.

But God does not leave us on our own. He says in verse 6, *"Do not be anxious about anything, but in everything, by prayer and petition, with thanksgiving, present your requests to God."*

When you were little you would run to momma who would wrap you in her loving arms. Well, that is what God wants to do for us. He wants us to run to the protection of His waiting arms. Nothing comes into your life that God can't handle. Just ask him! His words are faithful and true for everyone.

We need to run to Him. We must drop our earthly baggage at His precious feet and let Him hold us. There is no power on earth that can tear us out of the arms of Jesus. And after we have run to Jesus, after He has heard all our prayers and our heart's burdens *"the peace of God which transcends all understanding will guard your hearts and minds in Christ Jesus"* (verse 7).

The love of Christ is truly amazing! His peace passes all of our understanding. It is simply unlike anything we have ever known. Yes, there are many commands in God's Word for us to follow. In our own strength we cannot perfectly obey them. But nothing is impossible with God!

Rejoice!

♦

God's Plan

*"For whosoever shall call upon the name
of the Lord shall be saved."*
Romans 10:13 NASB

Christ came to preach and teach God's plan of salvation. He brought hope and healing. He made a way when we had no way. He is our Light and our Guide. He is the very breath we breathe. He is the very Son of God who loves us so much He gave His life for us.

There is no other way for us to have salvation except through Him. After we ask Jesus into our hearts, the blood He shed on Calvary's cross covers our sins. It is only through Jesus that we can have peace and fellowship with God our Creator.

Jesus, The anointed One, came to preach good news to the poor and afflicted.

Spiritually, I was poor and I was afflicted. He has forgiven me and brought me out of my sin and misery and brokenness. He will do the same for you.

My heart beats in anticipation of what God is going to do in my life. My heart is humbled and forever thankful for what God has already done. My friend, God wants this same peace and joy for you. Romans 10:9 says: *"That if thou shalt confess with thy mouth the Lord Jesus, and shalt believe in thine heart that God has raised Him from the dead, thou shalt be saved."* 1 John 5:13 tells us: *"These things have I written to you that believe on the name of the Son of God that you may know that ye have eternal life."*

Right now at this time in your life are you poor and afflicted? Does your soul ache with despair? Does the weight of your sin keep you from looking up into the face of the One who loves you and cares for you? Oh how He desires to heal and restore all who are poor in spirit and afflicted. Jesus our

108

only hope of salvation is waiting for you to trust Him. There is no other way to have forgiveness and salvation. Only Jesus can provide what you and I need. Won't you trust Him to lift that burden of sin and enable you to live a victorious life through Him? Call out to Him today. Do not delay. He will hear even the faintest whisper of your heart.

♦

Lovely Girls

"whatever is true, whatever is noble, whatever is right, whatever is pure, whatever is lovely.... .think about such things."
Philippians 4:8 NIV

Some of the best servants of Christ I know are young people. I thank God for them. Just the other day I listened as four lovely young ladies from our church youth group discussed their favorite books of the Bible and their favorite Bible passages. They talked about what they would read if they were struggling with something. What I overheard blessed my heart and encouraged me. Oh, how I wish I could turn back the clock of my life. I wish that I had known as a teenager the things these girls shared with each other that night. They will never know what a blessing they were to me. My life is better for knowing them. I love, admire, and respect the four of them very deeply. And I know that they are a sweet aroma to our Lord.

I love you, Bethel girls.

◆

A Thorn to Remember

"...There was given to me a thorn in the flesh....
to keep me from exalting myself."
2 Corinthians 12:7 NASB

Paul spoke of a thorn in the flesh that God had allowed into his life. It was that thing that would keep Paul humble and remind him all things come from Christ. And God chose not to remove Paul's thorn. Instead, He used it to draw Paul ever closer to himself. In verse 9 of 2 Corinthians 12, God reassures Paul that His grace is sufficient and His power perfected in weakness.

I have a "thorn" that keeps me grounded in Christ. Satan enjoys pulling it up from my pool of past sins. God is gracious to remind me that He has cast my sins into the depths of the sea of forgiveness where Satan cannot fish without my permission. I choose not to give him that pleasure.

Although I struggled for many years, I finally learned to trust God with all things—the past, present, and future things. He has never failed to bring me peace in my difficult hours when I have called to Him in prayer. Have you been there? Are you there right now? That thorn can either hold you back with needless suffering or cause you to draw closer to God. This second option is not a one-time fix. For the rest of our lives we will need to daily come before God's throne confessing our weaknesses and pleading for renewed strength.

Be at peace knowing that God's grace is indeed sufficient. In our weakest moments we are strong in Him.

We each have a thorn. We each know what it is to struggle. But what you may not realize is that even in our pain God is very near to us. Sometimes it is the deep sorrows of life that cause us to draw near to our Lord. That is when we will know true strength and peace and hope.

If we never had hardship, we would probably start believing we didn't need God. How sad would that be? How dangerous that would be!

111

When your thorn pierces your heart remember that God loves you with an amazing love.

Through Him, we can have a life in Christ that Paul speaks about in verse 10 where he testifies: *"Therefore I am well content with weaknesses, with insults, with distresses, with persecutions, with difficulties, for Christ's sake; for when I am weak, then, I am strong.*

God is good all the time. He is a God who knows us, who cares about us and will never leave us helpless. Allow God to give you the calm assurance, endurance, and certainty that He is able to bring you through any hardship you face. When you feel your thorn pressing against you, ask God for the grace and ability to use your suffering for His glory.

◆

Moving Past Our Normal

"For we are God's handiwork, created in Christ Jesus...."
Ephesians 2:10 NIV

We can hardly bear up under our affliction. Day after day we struggle with our pain and our fear and sadness. We're seeking the bright sunlight yet groping aimlessly in the darkness of our despair. Until one day the path of our journey comes to a detour. We come to where we have a choice. We can choose new life in Christ or we continue on the same lifeless path. Yet we find it hard to get off this path and onto the path God has prepared for us. We hold on to what may be hurting us as if we are a timid child clinging to the leg of his mother. We want to let go, but we are afraid to do so. Instead we cling to what we are familiar with... even if it hurts us.

This is not what God wants for us. We must not allow ourselves to remain in our affliction. Complacency seems too mild a word to describe our mindset regarding the daily cruelty we face. What keeps us bound to this pain? Heavy chains of negativity have been wrapped around us for so long we have succumbed to their weight. It is hard to stand, let alone step away from this burden. But God is waiting and nothing is too hard or too heavy for Him to take from us.

We can roll this weight from our hearts into the waiting arms of Jesus. He alone can lift it from us. No burden we carry is heavier than the weight of the cross. He carried that burden to His death! Because of His deep love for us, Jesus has already walked the path of rejection and humiliation on our behalf. He desires for us a different path, walking hand in hand with Him.

It is a fearful decision to leave behind the only thing we have ever known even if that very thing is destroying us.

But we must take that first step of faith towards God. There is a bright future ahead, a new beginning, a renewed hope. Break loose of those chains and step out in faith. Each day we have a choice. We can cling to God, our strength and protector or crawl back into our misery and loneliness.

Today can be the day you meet Jesus. He is the balm needed to heal your scars. God is good! He offers joy to you as well. God is waiting to bring you out of your desert of despair and into the soothing waters of His grace and forgiveness and restoration.

Yes, it is hard to let go of the only thing you have ever known, no matter how painful. But remember, as quickly as you let go of the pain, God is ready to reach out and catch you in His arms of mercy.

My friend, leave behind those things that hold you down. Why will you live in constant turmoil? You don't believe you deserve better. You believe it is normal to live in such bitterness. It is not! Step out into a new future with Jesus. He died so you and I can live. You are a unique creation formed by the hand of God and no one ever has the right to make you feel or believe otherwise. You are precious to Jesus and to me.

Father I have seen your grace poured out more this year in my life than ever before. You are an amazing God and I love you. My heart is so full it overflows into tears of deep gratitude and praise. When life seemed unbearable you lifted me up. You heard my cries for help and my prayers of deep agony. Only you knew the depths of my pain and despair and you delivered me, not only me but all who call on your precious name. You are only a whispered prayer away from whoever needs your healing touch. Thank you for the joy you have brought back into the hearts of those I love. Thank you for the faithfulness you've shown me. You have never failed me. You have never forsaken me. You are wonderful above anything I can imagine. You are God. I Praise you! In Jesus' name I pray.

◆

My Prayer

Father I lay down before you every dream, every desire of my heart. My prayer is that your precious blood would flow over me and cleanse me of all selfish motives and achievements. Father I dedicate my life fully to your service. I pray my heart, my mind and my soul would be open to your Holy Spirit's leading. My heart beats with a new rhythm, my lips sing a new song. Father you are all together lovely and I am a blessed woman that you would show such mercy and kindness to me. May all I do and every word written be for your glory. In Jesus' name I pray.

◆

23172004R10070

Made in the USA
Charleston, SC
14 October 2013